THE NEW TESTAMENT

Books by Oscar Cullmann
Published by The Westminster Press

THE NEW TESTAMENT: An Introduction for the General Reader

THE EARLY CHURCH (Abridged Edition)

CHRIST AND TIME: The Primitive Christian Conception of Time and History (Revised Edition)

THE CHRISTOLOGY OF THE NEW TESTAMENT (Revised Edition) (The New Testament Library)

PETER: Disciple, Apostle, Martyr (Second Revised and Expanded Edition) (Library of History and Doctrine)

The New Testament

An Introduction for the General Reader

By OSCAR CULLMANN

THE WESTMINSTER PRESS · PHILADELPHIA

PUBLISHED BY THE WESTMINSTER PRESS®
PHILADELPHIA, PENNSYLVANIA

PRINTED IN THE UNITED STATES OF AMERICA

CONTENTS

Preface to the English Translation

This small book presented now to the English-speaking public was written for the French collection *Que sais-je?*, a series popularizing general knowledge. In a strictly limited number of pages, intended for cultured, but not specialized, readers, this collection gives the present situation in all areas of human knowledge, in a language within the reach of all. Any purely technical discussion must be kept to the very minimum. We thus had to grapple with the difficulty of explaining, in the 128 pages of the French edition, all the literary and historical problems brought up by each of the twenty-seven books of the New Testament and their collection, without omitting anything essential. On the other hand, since for the general public the New Testament is probably here envisaged from the scientific viewpoint for the first time in many cases, we decided not to limit ourselves to the questions of authorship and date usually dealt with exclusively by the big " introductions to the New Testament." Rather, we at least touched on the discussion of their theological content; thus our task was all the harder.

If we did not back off from this difficulty, it was because we are convinced that it is necessary to inject an elementary knowledge of the problems regarding the formation and content of the New Testament into the domain called " general culture " required from everyone. As a matter of fact, we have often noticed in people very cultured in other respects an astonishing ignorance in this area.

It was both this conviction and the extraordinary success with which the French edition has met that made us decide to bring out this small book in America also, although there is no lack of technical works on the science of the New Testament in English.

Finally, we would voice two desires. If perchance this work should come under the examination of specialists, let them remember that it was not written for them, and take into consideration the limits which we had to observe because of its nature. As for those for whom it is intended, we hope that it will cause them to read or reread the New Testament itself.

O. C.

Chamonix,
August, 1967

Introduction

Within the body of early Christian literature, twenty-seven books have found a privileged place. They won acceptance (and such was the case, much more so than simply an arbitrary choice), and little by little they were gathered together, standardized in one collection, and considered to be Holy Scripture (see below, Part Three: " The Formation of the New Testament Canon "). Christians already had a group of writings available that they considered holy: the Bible inherited from Judaism. Later, they called it " The Old Testament " and added to it the twenty-seven new books which received the name " The New Testament."

It is this New Testament which we are going to study in this book. Without denying the genuine interest that the entire body of early Christian literature offers, we believe that these twenty-seven books must be studied in their own right, if for no other reason, because of the exceptional part they have taken right up to our day in the history of the church as well as in that of the world.

Not only has the New Testament been, and still is, the Christian code of faith, not only has it inspired, and inspires still, many heroic lives, famous or hidden, but it has also left its mark on the individual and social ethics of civilizations, on their literature and on their art.

PART ONE: HISTORY
OF THE NEW TESTAMENT TEXT

Today, when a reader leafs through the New Testament in one of the modern editions of the Bible, he finds a text that is meant to be clear, both in typography and in style, and he cannot realize the diversity and the complexity of the documents on which the printed text is based, or the enormous difficulties that had to be met with in bringing to light, deciphering, and evaluating these basic documents.

Chapter 1

The Basic Documents

We have no original document of the New Testament, only copies. The oldest *complete* manuscripts that we have do not reach back beyond the fourth century; more ancient fragments aside, about three hundred years separate the original writing from the text as it has been preserved.

Such a lapse of time could bring up doubts about the authenticity of these texts. It is true that from one copy to another deformations and errors managed to creep in and obtain acceptance. However, it must not be forgotten that the New Testament, as soon as it was recognized as Holy Scripture, was recopied with the scrupulous minuteness that is inspired by respect for holy things. We

must also note that the separation between the original
and the first preserved text is, even if we disregard the
fragments, smaller for the New Testament writings than
for the other writings of antiquity. For example, the oldest manuscript of the works of Aeschylus (525–456 B.C.)
dates only from about the year 1000.

The conditions in which the text was handed down
were not, therefore, as unfavorable as may seem at first
glance, and no exaggerated skepticism from the histori-
ans in this regard could be justified.

Evaluating the distance separating the New Testament writings from the events to which they bear witness
is another problem; we will examine this problem for
each one of the twenty-seven books in the second part of
this study. We will start off with a classification of the
basic documents.

I. The Manuscripts

The New Testament manuscripts can be classed according to the material they are made from, or according
to the type of characters used. This classification helps
in dating them.

The manuscripts are either papyri or parchments.

A *papyrus* is made up of strips of pith from the papyrus
(a kind of reed with a triangular stem, from the family of
Cyperaceae, about as large as a man's arm and seven and
a half to fifteen feet high). These strips are finely cut and
glued together in crosswise layers, to form sheets which
are then attached end to end and rolled up on a rod. The
roll thus formed is called in Greek *biblos* (whence the
word " Bible ") and can be over thirty feet long.

The New Testament papyri are the oldest basic documents that we have. Most of them come from the third

century (one papyrus, discovered in 1935, must even be dated from the first part of the second century). Although they furnish us with only text fragments, these documents are valuable evidence for the text precisely because of their ancientness. Today we have seventy-two of them, designated in the critical editions by P^1, P^2, and so on.

A *parchment* is an animal skin, usually a sheepskin, a goatskin, or a calfskin, treated and cut up into leaves (the word "parchment" is the corruption of *pergamēnē*, for this procedure is supposed to have originated in Pergamum) which are placed one above another to make up, not a roll, but a "volume" (in Greek, *teuchos*, whence our word "Pentateuch" to designate the first five books of the Old Testament).

Parchments containing New Testament texts do not date from earlier than the fourth century, but, generally speaking, they provide us with complete texts of the New Testament. Because of easily imaginable deterioration, the beginning and the end of the text sometimes lack the leaves that formed the cover.

All these documents are written in Greek, but the Greek is no longer classical. Its morphology is simplified and deformed, the syntax is often irregular, and the vocabulary has evolved under various influences, especially that of the Hebrew language. (This Greek commonly spoken throughout the Empire is called Koine, *common* language.)

The oldest New Testament manuscripts are written in *capital letters,* or uncials. There are presently 242 of them. The critical editions designate them by capital letters.

The manuscripts in *cursive script* (today 2,570 of them are known) date, at the very earliest, from the ninth century. They must not be completely left aside, because the copyists of the ninth, tenth, or eleventh centuries were perhaps copying manuscripts in capital letters that we no longer possess. The critical editions designate them with Arabic numerals.

All these manuscripts are rather hard to read. No space whatsoever separates the words, sentences, and paragraphs, and we can find neither accents nor punctuation marks.

Variants are found from one text to another. They are often the result of involuntary mistakes: the copyist skipped a word; or, on the contrary, wrote it twice in a row; or again, part of a sentence was omitted inadvertently because, in the manuscript being recopied, it was placed between two identical words. Sometimes the corrections were on purpose: either the copyist ventured to correct the text according to his own ideas, or else he tried to harmonize the text being copied with a parallel (especially for the first three Gospels), in order to reduce, more or less cleverly, the differences. As the New Testament writings stood out from the rest of the early Christian literature and were looked upon as Holy Scripture, the copyists hesitated more and more to venture such corrections of their predecessors: they thought they were copying the authentic text and thus fixed the variants. Lastly, a copyist would sometimes annotate the text in the margin to explain an obscure passage. The next copyist, thinking that such a sentence which he found written in the margin had been accidentally forgotten by his predecessor, believed it necessary to reintroduce this marginal annotation into the text. Thus the new text occasionally became even more obscure.

The evaluation of the variants is delicate. One of the main principles in this evaluation is that of the *lectio difficilior,* of the more difficult reading: between two readings of the same text, the reading that presents the most difficulty, either because of its irregular grammatical form or because of the ideas it conveys, just might be the authentic reading, since the copyists' corrections always tended to eliminate or reduce the incomprehensible, suspicious, or shocking items in a text. One more important factor in the evaluation of the manuscripts is left: age.

Six manuscripts in capitals are very important. The first is the Codex Vaticanus (designated by " B " in the critical editions), so named because it is kept in the Vatican library. From the fourth century, it is the oldest of the parchment manuscripts. The Codex Sinaiticus (designated by " א "), discovered in a monastery on Mt. Sinai in the nineteenth century, sold in 1933 by the Soviet government to the British Museum in London, is also to be dated from the fourth century. The Codex Alexandrinus (designated by " A "), brought from Alexandria to England in the seventeenth century, also kept at the British Museum, is dated from the fifth century. The Codex Ephraemi Rescriptus (designated by " C ") is a palimpsest, that is, the first text, a manuscript of the New Testament from the fifth century, was erased in the twelfth century by a copyist who used the parchment for copying works of Ephraem of Syria. Fortunately, the first text was not entirely removed and can still be read under the medieval text by experienced eyes (arduous work, made easier today by modern technical procedures). This manuscript is kept in Paris, at the Bibliothèque Nationale. These first four manuscripts differ from one another only in " variants " of details.

Two other codices (designated by " D ") show a great number of particularly well known readings that vary from the four preceding manuscripts. They are both from the sixth century. The first is the Codex Bezae Cantabrigiensis and it owes its name to the fact that it belonged, as did the second, to Theodore Beza, friend of Calvin, and that its owner gave it to Cambridge in 1581. Written in two columns, the first containing the Greek text, the second the Latin translation, it includes only the four Gospels and the book of The Acts of the Apostles. An example of the interesting variants of the Codex Bezae is furnished by these words of Jesus reported by this manuscript only: " The same day, Jesus saw a man working on the Sabbath day, and said to him, ' Man, if you know what you are doing, you are happy! If you know not, you are cursed, and you are a transgressor of the Law! ' " (Luke 6:5). The second manuscript, which contains the epistles and is entirely similar to that of Cambridge, takes its name from the place where it was discovered: Clermont. The Codex Claromontanus is now kept in the Bibliothèque Nationale in Paris.

II. THE TRANSLATIONS

A second group of documents comes next made up of the ancient *translations*. They are especially interesting because they are older than the Greek manuscripts we possess. Some of them, in fact, date from the second century and were prepared from manuscripts that have now been lost and that are older than those mentioned above. They are, therefore, chronologically closer to the originals.

A well-known translation in the West is that of Jerome in the fourth century, called the Vulgate. But we also have a good number of manuscripts (about forty-four) of Latin translations anterior to the Vulgate, which are therefore more valuable and have received the collective title Vetus Itala. (In the critical editions they are designated by small letters.)

The *Syriac translations* owe their exceptional interest not only to their ancientness but also to the fact that Syriac is a language close to the Palestinian Aramaic spoken by Jesus and his associates. Several authors of the New Testament wrote in Greek what they were thinking in Aramaic, and the Syriac translations can help us in certain cases to understand better what they meant to say. The most famous Syriac translation is the Peshitta ("simple") from the fifth century (its sigla: syr[p]), but two others are also known which are older and more valuable: the Sinaitic Syriac version (syr[s]) and the Curetonian Syriac version (syr[c]).

Lastly we have the *Coptic translations* (Coptic was the language of the Christians of Egypt), which are worthy of great attention. Some of them have just recently been discovered.

III. THE QUOTATIONS

A third group of documents is formed by the quotations from the New Testament that can be found scattered throughout the writings of the fathers of the church. Rare in the second century, their number grew ever larger as the New Testament, recognized as Holy Scripture, began to command absolute authority.

These quotations have the advantage of indicating to us the geographical origin of a certain form of the text, but they must be used with caution in criticism. For when a passage quoted by one of the fathers differs from the text of the New Testament generally used in the country where he lived, this difference is not necessarily a true variant, evidence of an unknown manuscript, but may simply result from a quotation made from memory.

Chapter 2

Classification of the Basic Documents: "The Families of Texts"

Confronted with the various texts that we have just enumerated, the critics, who have been concentrating on this kind of research (see Chapter 3, below) since the nineteenth century, noticed that the same variants are reproduced in a series of manuscripts of entirely different ages and origins. They were led to the supposition that these manuscripts derived from a common type. It was thus possible to establish several *families of texts,* and to obtain:

1. *The Syrian text,* represented by the great majority of ancient manuscripts. This text, greatly adulterated, the result of the revisions of a more ancient text, is the worst. Widely spread in Europe from the sixteenth century on, thanks to the printing press, it became everywhere the "received" text. (See Chapter 3, below.)

2. *The Western text,* although the appellation is not altogether correct,[1] originated from the Antioch region. From there, beginning even before the third century, it spread throughout the Christian world by following the trade routes and was established in the West, especially in Rome, where Justin Martyr was acquainted with it, in

---

1 Perhaps it could be called the "Syro-Latin" text, because of its origin and spread.

Lyons, taken there by Irenaeus, and in Africa. The Codex Bezae, the Codex Claromontanus, the Latin versions, and some Western fathers of the church provide the most representative evidences for this family. In spite of a certain bent for secondary paraphrasing, they must not be eliminated from consideration for the establishing of the original text.

3. *The neutral text*, so called because it is relatively free from ulterior alterations and because its chief characteristic is that of being fairly pure. It is especially represented by the Codex Vaticanus and the Codex Sinaiticus. While it was in Alexandria, it underwent slight alterations tending to make it more correct, and the " Alexandrian " text, only a variant of the greater family, was born.

Although this classification enables us to pass an *a priori* judgment on the worth of the variants, each case must undergo an individual examination taking into account all the variants.

Chapter 3

History of the Printed Text

The New Testament was one of the first books to be printed. One of the earliest editions of the Greek text is due to the initiative of Cardinal Jiménez, Archbishop of Toledo, deceased in 1517, who had a polyglot Bible printed at Alcalá (in Latin, Complutum). In this Bible, called Complutensis, which did not come out until 1520, the Greek New Testament, already finished and printed in 1514, took up the fifth volume. It is difficult to determine the manuscripts on which this text was established.

Froben, printer in Basel, had asked the humanist Erasmus as early as 1515 to prepare a Greek text of the New Testament for publication. Froben wanted to bring out his edition before that of the Alcalá Bible, and so Erasmus' work, published in 1516, was hasty and mismanaged. The humanist used poor manuscripts (cursives and late Syrian text) from the eleventh and twelfth centuries, kept in Basel. Following editions were corrected, but they never attained real scientific worth. Luther translated the New Testament from a reprinting of the second edition of 1519.

Taking as their basic text that of Erasmus, compared with the Complutensis and a dozen manuscripts (including the Codex Bezae), the printers Robert Estienne

(1503–1559) and his son Henri (1528–1578) published four editions of the Greek New Testament: 1546, 1549, 1550, 1551. For the first time in this last edition the division of the chapters into verses appeared. (The division of the text into chapters goes back to the thirteenth century.) This is a defective text, but it provided the basis for the rest of the sixteenth-century printed editions, for example, the nine editions published by Theodore Beza (1519–1605), whose first edition came out in 1565. This same text was adopted again in the seventeenth century by the Elzevir brothers, printers. Thanks to their prestige, it was widely spread, until it became the " received text." The origin of this appellation was the preface to the second Elzevir edition in which the following words can be read: " So now you have the text received by all." Its unmerited authority led to the saying, " *Textus receptus sed non recipiendus.*" (" The received text which is not to be received.")

It was only at the beginning of the nineteenth century that editions began to appear which applied a critical method, taking into account the history of the text and the relations between the different families of manuscripts. After the preparatory work of Simon (died, 1712), Bengel (died, 1752), and Wettstein (died, 1754), this method was ushered in by Griesbach (died, 1812). Among the principal editors who have followed him we shall mention Lachmann (died, 1851), Tischendorf (died, 1874), Westcott (died, 1901), Hort (died, 1892), von Soden (died, 1914), and Eberhard Nestle (died, 1913). Today the most commonly used text for the exegetical study of the New Testament is that established by Nestle.[2] It is a composite text, that is, it does not corre-

[2] Later revised editions of this text have been brought out. After the death of Eberhard Nestle, his son Erwin Nestle and, later

spond to any one manuscript, but combines, as in a mosaic, the texts that have been established by the leading modern editors. A veritable code of signs, placed in the text and referring to notes at the bottom of the page, enables one to see in every case from which manuscript the reading chosen by the editor has been taken, and the variants offered by the other manuscripts for this particular case.

The most complete edition is still that of Tischendorf (eighth edition, 1869 ff.). But a new edition is being prepared which will take into account all the manuscripts discovered since that date. An international team is working on it. This edition will be called the *New Critical Apparatus of the Greek New Testament,* and the first volume brought out will contain the Gospel of Luke.

---

on, Kurt Aland kept up his work; now the most recent edition is the twenty-fifth, which came out in 1963. A comparable edition, more commonly used by Catholic scholars, is that published by A. Merk (seventh edition, 1951).

PART TWO: THE WRITINGS OF THE NEW TESTAMENT

Chapter 4

The Narrative Writings

In a literary history of the books of the New Testament, we should proceed chronologically, starting with the Pauline epistles, which we know of a certainty were written before the Gospels.

However, several of the twenty-seven New Testament writings can only be dated uncertainly, and we do not know in what order to arrange them. We feel, therefore, that it is best to follow, roughly speaking, the traditional order and to begin our analytical study by the narrative writings: the four Gospels and the book of The Acts of the Apostles.

I. THE GOSPEL AND THE GOSPELS

The Greek term *euangelion,* which is translated " gospel," comes from classical Greek. It meant, for example, in Homer and Plutarch, the reward given to the messenger for his message; in the plural, the thank offerings presented to the gods for a bit of good news. In a wider sense, it took the meaning, in Aristophanes for example, of the message itself, and then the contents of the message, the good news that is announced. Thus the birthday of the emperor Augustus, called god and savior, is celebrated as "the beginning for the world of the good news he brought." The Greek translation of the Old Testament, called the Septuagint, also uses this word to designate favorable messages. Among the early Christians, the *euangelion* was first of all the good news of salvation brought about in Jesus Christ. It is in this sense that we speak of the four Gospels and that the authors to whom we attribute them are called Evangelists: Matthew, Mark, Luke, and John.

The Gospels form a literary genre in their own right, which does not resemble in the least the genres known in classical literature. Their biographical appearance must not be permitted to mask what they are meant to be above all — the witness of the community borne for Jesus Christ, Son of God and Savior of men.

There are four Gospels, and this fact presents a double problem.

The *theological* problem, already sensed in antiquity, is as follows: Why were four testimonies necessary for the same facts? Could one not harmonize the four narratives to fuse them into one Life of Jesus? Some have tried, from the very beginning of Christianity, to reduce this plurality. Tatian, in the second century, composed a Gospel harmony, the Diatessaron ("by four," with "only one" implied); still in the second century, Marcion radically did away with three out of four Gospels, keeping only the Gospel of Luke.

The Christian church, refusing these attempts for artificial unification, received the four Gospels side by side, but gave them titles which indicate clearly that it is a question of four testimonies dealing with one event and one person, one item of good news heard in different and complementary ways, a unique, tetramorphic Gospel *according to* Matthew, *according to* Mark, *according to* Luke, *according to* John.

But this plurality also presents a *literary* problem. The first three Gospels — Matthew, Mark, and Luke — show a certain unity with one another when compared with the fourth, John. Everything in these three takes place within the same chronological and geographical limits: Jesus' ministry extends over one year; it starts in Galilee and ends in Judea with the passion. John, on the contrary, extends this ministry over two or three years, and places it directly in Judea and occasionally in Galilee.

The outline in the first three Gospels is so similar that they can be copied in three columns and read in parallel at a glance, whence the name " Synoptic " Gospels. This term, used for the first time in the eighteenth century by Griesbach, is derived from the Greek *sunoraō,* which means " to see together," " to see from the same vantage point."

We have, therefore, before us the " Synoptic Problem ": How can one explain the relationship of these three Gospels and, on the other hand, the differences which yet exist among them?

The Synoptics are alike, we would be tempted to say, because they deal with the same material; but this explanation is not adequate, since it should be valid for the fourth Gospel as well, which is not the case. Even more, it does not take into account the sameness of the general arrangement of the scattered materials used in the Synoptics. For each Evangelist had at his disposal only isolated narratives and words of Jesus that were transmitted by oral tradition; he could, therefore, construct his outline as he wished. If, in spite of this, there is a roughly identical outline, one must consequently admit a mutual dependence of these three texts.

On the other hand, the Synoptics are not without differences. Certain episodes are found in only two Gospels, others in just one. The childhood of Jesus is told differently in Matthew than in Luke and is not even mentioned in Mark. Jesus' appearances after his resurrection are situated by Luke in Judea, by Matthew in Galilee. The great sermons that can be read in Matthew are not to be found in Mark. The resurrection of the son of the widow of Nain, the episode of the forgiving of the woman taken in sin, the parable of the good Samaritan, the story of Martha and Mary, etc., are found only in Luke, and within the common outline it was necessary to interpolate a framework for these materials. Even more, within the parallel texts themselves differences abound.

In the past, several solutions have been proposed to solve this literary problem. The very fact that there are so many demonstrates that none of them is really satisfactory. It is essentially a question of hypotheses that do not solve the whole problem. We will enumerate only the principal ones. The last, called the " two-source hypothesis," is still today the most widely accepted, although it raises difficulties, as do the others.

1. *Hypothesis of usage.* Here is how this hypothesis is stated: The three Synoptics were all used mutually, and in the course of this process modifications were introduced. This solution, found for the first time in this form in Augustine's writings, is traditional. Matthew is supposed to be the first Gospel written, Mark made a résumé of Matthew, and Luke used both of them. Whence the traditional order of the Gospels: Matthew, Mark, Luke. Other more modern hypotheses bear a resemblance to this one. As early as 1789, Griesbach proposed a comparable theory, except that he put Luke before Mark; according to him, Mark therefore used Matthew and Luke.

With a different order, the solution was taken up again in 1835 by Lachmann, and in 1838 by Wilke.

2. *Hypothesis of a primitive gospel.* According to this hypothesis, the three Synoptics go back to a common source of Aramaic origin which is no longer extant, and each one of the writers used this source in his own way. The name of Lessing (1778) has become attached to this hypothesis. Eichhorn adopted this solution with his own modifications (1804).

3. *Hypothesis of narratives.* This hypothesis attributes a written prehistory to the Gospels. Small pieces (*diēgēseis*) are supposed to have been written first — narratives of the passion, narratives of miracles, collections of the sayings of Jesus. Each one of the Evangelists later on combined in his own way these different items. This theory, sustained by Schleiermacher in 1817, already anticipates and even surpasses in many ways, the very latest explanations which we will treat in a moment.

4. *Hypothesis of oral tradition.* This hypothesis goes back to Herder (1797). According to it, oral tradition was fixed quite early, and the Evangelists limited themselves to drawing from this common tradition, each in his own way. Here again, this theory anticipates the most recent evolution of the history of the problem.

5. *Hypothesis of two sources* (complemented by the recent studies on the formation of tradition). The hypothesis of two sources (exposed by Holtzmann in 1863) is really a combination of the hypotheses of usage and of the early gospel which has been lost. Matthew and Luke used Mark independently, the latter being therefore the oldest of the three, as well as a common source now lost. This source is supposed to have contained especially the sayings of Jesus (*logia*). This hypothesis, rejected by several (Zahn, Schlatter), from its very beginning won the

acceptance of the scholars.[3] However, in the light of more recent study, it must, in any case, be corrected and made more precise as far as several points are concerned that are still problematical. For example, Was the Gospel of Mark used by Matthew and Luke exactly the one that we know today? Different indications point to a "Proto-Mark." On the other hand, it is not sure that the common source was unique and precisely complete. There were probably several collections of *logia*, as the recently discovered Gnostic Gospel of Thomas would seem to prove.

But we must take into special account the fact that the Synoptic Gospels are to a great extent only spokesmen for the early Christian community. It is this community which fixed the oral tradition. For thirty or forty years the Gospel existed almost exclusively in oral form; now, oral tradition handed down principally sayings and isolated narratives. The Evangelists spun their own connections, each as he wished, each with his own personality and his individual theological concerns, between the sayings and narratives received from the ambient tradition. The grouping of Jesus' words, as well as the sequence of the narratives accomplished by rather vague joining phrases, such as " after this," " immediately," and so forth — in a word, the " framework" of the Synoptics — is purely literary and has no historical foundation.

Finally, we must note that the needs of preaching, teaching, and worship rather than a biographical interest guided the early community in fixing this tradition of the life of Jesus. The apostles illustrated the truths of the Christian faith they were preaching by recounting events from the life of Jesus, and it was their sermons that enabled the narratives to take on a fixed form. The sayings

[3] Although, again, variants or different solutions are still being proposed (cf. Streeter, Vaganay, Farmer, etc.).

of Jesus were in particular handed down in the catechetical teaching of the early church. Recently, Swedish scholars (Harald Riesenfeld, Birger Gerhardsson) have emphasized how the disciples of the rabbis learned by heart the words of their masters.

What we have just proposed is supported by the studies of the *Formgeschichte* school, as it is called. Really, at the beginning it was not a question of a "school" proper, but of the convergence of several schools, which appeared between 1919 and 1922. The purpose of the authors of these schools was to study the history of the formation and of the forms ("genres" — this is the meaning of the German word *Formgeschichte*) of the Gospel.

Martin Dibelius, Karl Ludwig Schmidt, and Rudolf Bultmann applied this method to the Gospels, a method which we might call paleontological. It allows us to determine the laws and the circumstances (*Sitz im Leben*) that brought forth the different parts of the oral tradition of the Gospel.[4]

We still have to define the personal contribution of each Evangelist, a study that the scholars have especially taken up since the last war (*Redaktiongeschichte*), by studying: (1) *the choice* made by the Evangelist within the tradition itself; (2) *the outline* within which the chosen items were arranged. This literary study will enable us to isolate in each Gospel the particular ideas that each author has of the "Gospel."

II. The Gospel According to Matthew

In the traditional order, The Gospel According to Matthew opens the New Testament. This is justified in the sense that out of the four Evangelists Matthew tries the

[4] See our articles on *Formgeschichte* in the *Revue d'Histoire et de Philosophie religieuses* (1925), pp. 459–477 and pp. 564–579.

hardest to stay in the Old Testament line of thought. He
bridges the expectation of the Messianic Kingdom, whose
coming is proclaimed in the prophetic books of the Old
Testament, and the coming of Jesus Christ, presented by
the New Testament as the answer to this expectation.

1. *Originality and Origin of The Gospel According to
Matthew.* The First Gospel is very systematic and the
writing is well thought out. Matthew groups the narratives and maxims by subjects (for example, chs. 5 to 7:
the law; ch. 11: John the Baptist; ch. 23: the Pharisees).
He applies his attention in a special way to the traditions
concerning the opinion and attitude of Jesus before the
Jewish law.

He also endeavors to show that Jesus did not come to
reject the Old Testament but to bring it to its goal, to its
fulfillment. He chooses from the oral tradition some of
Jesus' words such as these: " Do not think that I have
come to abolish the law or the prophets. [That is, the entire Old Testament.] I have not come to abolish, but to
fulfill. Verily I say unto you: heaven and earth shall not
pass away, not an iota, not a crossing of a letter of the
law shall pass away before all is fulfilled " (Matt. 5: 17-
18). Then follows a discussion in which Jesus takes one
by one several of the precepts of the Jewish law in order
to teach his disciples not their transgression but their fulfillment, not formally but totally, radically (" but I say
unto you . . .").

Moreover, for Matthew the fulfillment of the Old Testament is accomplished, not only by Jesus' doctrine but
by his very person in the events of his life; thus, after recounting the birth of Jesus, he adds, " All this took place
to fulfil what the Lord had spoken by the prophet "
(Matt. 1:22; other texts, for example, chs. 21:4 ff.; 26:54;
27:9; 13:35).

This insistence on the Old Testament is an echo of the bitter discussions with which, especially during the first century, Judaism and Christians of Jewish extraction were confronted. Matthew's choice of narratives from the life of Jesus is another evidence of this tendency. Perhaps he used, from among already written documents, kinds of anthologies of Old Testament texts applied to Christ. Although we have none of them today, it has been proven that such collections did exist and they are usually designated by the term *testimonia* (cf. the studies of Rendel Harris and P. Prigent). According to certain scholars, such as Stendahl, we should rather speak of a Christian rabbinical school of Matthew, which spent its time scrutinizing the Old Testament to discover in it predictions concerning Christ.

2. *What do we know about the milieu of its origin?* The author of the First Gospel is a Jew converted to Christianity, and he lives in a Jewish Christian community that is endeavoring to separate itself from its attachments with Judaism while maintaining continuity with the Old Testament. Its special interests, the general tone of this Gospel, suggest the existence of a tension-filled situation. The vocabulary indicates that the author is a Jew and that he is writing to those who, although they speak Greek, are acquainted with Jewish customs [5] and the Aramaic language.[6]

But where should this Jewish Christian community be situated? Because of the lack of decisive arguments, Jerusalem, Galilee, Antioch, Alexandria, or one of the great cities of the Phoenician coastal region of Syria (Tyre,

---

[5] He alludes to them without considering it necessary to explain them (cf. Matt. 15:2 ff.).

[6] In Matt. 5:22, he does not take the trouble to translate the word *raca*.

Sidon, Ptolemais), or perhaps a city within the boundary of northern Palestine and Syria such as Caesarea of Philippi or Damascus, have all been proposed. For the time being it is impossible to make a pronouncement.

When was this Gospel produced in this Jewish Christian community? We can rest assured that it is the fruit of long years of community experiences. A detail in the parable of the wedding feast, in ch. 22:7, can lead us to suppose that the First Gospel was written after the Jewish rebellion and the burning of Jerusalem ordered by Titus in 70. The writing of the First Gospel should therefore be dated from around the year 80.

Tradition (and not the text itself, which does not even give such a hint) has ascribed this Gospel to Matthew, the "tax collector" whose conversion is mentioned in ch. 9:9 (the other two Synoptics call him Levi) and who became one of the disciples according to ch. 10:3. But nothing enables us to confirm this tradition which brings up difficulties, especially if we admit that the author used the Gospel of Mark, the latter not being a disciple of Jesus. We can only say that examination of the text leads us to attribute it readily to a Jew of Palestinian origin who spoke Greek and who was converted to the new faith. Did the author use an Aramaic source written by Matthew, and if such is the case, was this writing a complete gospel or just a collection of Jesus' sayings (*logia*), as some admit, basing their opinion on a report by Papias (140) concerning a work written "in Hebrew" by Matthew? This is simply a hypothesis.

3. *The Message of The Gospel According to Matthew.* Fifty-one times Matthew uses the Greek word *basileia,* which can be translated "kingdom," or "reign." "Kingdom of God," "Kingdom of Heaven," "the Father's kingdom," or "kingdom" — all these expressions reveal a

Jewish way of thinking. Judaism at the time of Jesus spoke of the Kingdom of God that would be established in the future, and certain other fervent circles were waiting for the reign of the Messiah as an imminent reality.

The Kingdom of Heaven announced by Matthew is future. To be convinced one would only have to read ch. 13:43: " *Then* the righteous will shine like the sun in the kingdom of their Father," or ch. 25:34: " *Then* the King will say to those at his right hand, ' Come, O blessed of my Father, inherit the kingdom prepared for you from the foundation of the world.' " (See also chs. 7:21; 8:11; 16:28.) Like the Promised Land toward which the people of Israel in the Old Testament were marching, the Kingdom is the goal of the believers, a " territory " they will possess, and into which they will enter. The Kingdom is therefore a *future reality*, claim such authors as Alfred Loisy or Albert Schweitzer whose theory is called " consistent eschatology." [7]

But Matthew also preaches a reign that begins with the coming of Jesus Christ. Read, for example, ch. 12:28: " But if it is by the Spirit of God that I cast out demons, then the kingdom of God has come upon you." (See also chs. 4; 17; 5:3, 10; 11:3 ff., 12.) The Kingdom is therefore a *present reality*, claim the theologians of " realized eschatology " such as C. H. Dodd.

These two theories are extreme and partial. In fact, according to Matthew the Kingdom has already been ushered in by the coming of Jesus Christ, but it is *not yet* fully manifested as it will be by his coming at the end of time. Believers now consider themselves to be in the intermediary time between this " already " and the " not yet "; they are already (and the world with them) under

[7] Eschatology: a word derived from Greek (*eschata*, " the last things ") which designates the doctrine of last real events.

the reign of Christ, but they are still waiting for his glorious Kingdom. The parables of ch. 13, and particularly
the parable of the good seed and the tares, clearly point
out the double reality of this Kingdom (vs. 24-30 and 36-
43); the sowing has been done, but we are not yet in
harvesttime.

The announcement of the Kingdom and the fulfillment
of the Old Testament by Jesus Christ are, in addition to
the concern for putting together a new individual and social ethics making truly manifest the newness of the gospel, the dominant factors of the particular message addressed to us by the first Evangelist.

III. The Gospel According to Mark

The Second Gospel was for a long time considered to
be a résumé of the first, and Bossuet called Mark "the
divine abbreviator." In fact, as we have said, everything
leads us to believe that Mark is the oldest of the four.

The transmittal of its text presents an oddity at the
end. In the two oldest manuscripts of the New Testament, the Codex Vaticanus and the Codex Sinaiticus (as
well as the Sinaitic Syriac version and other sources), the
Gospel ends abruptly in ch. 16:8: " And they [the women
who had found Christ's tomb empty] said nothing to any
one, for they were afraid." More recent Greek manuscripts and certain versions have added here a conclusion dealing with Christ's appearances, which is not from
Mark but drawn from the other Gospels. The textual
problem that comes up here is the following: Does v. 8
mark the authentic ending of the Gospel, or has the original ending been lost by accident or done away with on
purpose? According to one recent hypothesis, the lost
ending of Mark contained the story of an appearance of

the Resurrected One to Peter, traces of this story being found in John, ch. 21.

1. *Who is Mark and what is the origin of his Gospel?* Tradition gives Mark as the author of the Second Gospel, and there is no serious reason to doubt this attribution, although the text itself does not speak of the author. In fact, if someone had invented an author for this Gospel, he would have chosen to attribute it to an apostle to give it more authority. It was to cover this writing with apostolic authority that Christian tradition, after 150, claimed that the apostle Peter, in whose company Mark was to be found according to I Peter 5:13, was its guarantor, and that Mark was only Peter's secretary. This sponsorship may seem suspicious to some, but the objection can be made that Matthew and Luke would not perhaps have used this Gospel as they did if they had not known that it was actually based on the teachings of an apostle.

It seems reasonable to identify Mark with " John whose other name was Mark," whom we hear about several times throughout the New Testament. According to Acts 12:12, the mother of Mark opened up her house in Jerusalem to a part of the community for prayer. Mark was the companion of the apostle Paul, if we accept Acts 12:25; 13:5, 13; 15:37-39; Col. 4:10; and perhaps he also worked with the apostle Peter with whom he was acquainted according to Acts 12:12 and I Peter 5:13.

Was he an eyewitness of at least a part of Jesus' life? This is sustained by an ancient tradition, which perhaps confirms the curious verse which we find in his Gospel (and there only) in the very middle of the passion story: " A young man followed him, with nothing but a linen cloth about his body; and they seized him, but he left the linen cloth and ran away naked " (Mark 14:51-52). This anecdote, void of importance for the events of the passion, and void of theological interest, could lead one to suppose that the young man was Mark, and that he wanted to include, by this personal memory, a mark of authenticity, an " anonymous signature," proving that he was an eyewitness.

An examination of the vocabulary, style, and ideas of the Second Gospel will enable us to expose more clearly its milieu. The important role attributed to Galilee and numerous Aramaic sentence constructions corroborate the hypothesis that the author was of Jewish extraction [8]; but we also find Latinisms in his text. He transcribes Latin words into Greek.[9] It is, therefore, not impossible that he wrote his Gospel in Rome. Moreover, he is writing to Christians no longer living in Palestine, and he takes care to explain to them the Aramaic expressions he uses, for example, in ch. 5:41: " Taking her by the hand he [Jesus] said to her, ' Talitha cumi '; which means, ' Little girl, I say unto you, arise ' "; the same is true for Jewish customs, as in ch. 7:3-4: " For the Pharisees, and all the Jews, do not eat unless they [carefully] wash their hands . . . ; and when they come from the market place, they do not eat unless they purify themselves; and there are many other traditions which they observe, the washing of cups and pots and vessels of bronze."

Finally, a profound influence from the apostle Paul's thought can be easily recognized in the Second Gospel, also suggested by the book of The Acts of the Apostles,

---

[8] For example, the periphrastic conjugation with a present participle: " Jesus was preceding them " (Mark 10:32), and the use of " behold " at the beginning of certain sentences (chs. 2:24; 3:32; etc.).

[9] He speaks of *legiōn* (Latin: *legio* = legion in Mark 5:9), of *spekoulatōr* (Latin: *speculator* = Roman soldier responsible for guarding prisoners in ch. 6:27), or *dēnarion* (Latin: *denarius* = denarius in v. 37), etc.

which makes Mark the collaborator of Paul in his missionary journeys. The Evangelist is probably, therefore, a Jew transplanted into a "Romanized" Christian community (Rome?) after a long period of missionary work among the heathen, largely as a collaborator of the apostle Paul.

If we take into account the allusions, too brief we must admit, to the destruction of the Jerusalem Temple, his Gospel can be dated approximately from the year 70.

2. *The message of the Second Gospel.* From the very beginning, the Gospel of Mark gives its purpose: "The beginning of the gospel of Jesus Christ, Son of God" (ch. 1:1). What comes after is meant to be a testimony borne to the divine Sonship of Jesus Christ.

The appellation "Son of God" applied to Jesus is not peculiar to the Second Gospel, but what is particular and meaningful is that although Mark uses this term much less frequently than Matthew, he gives it full meaning by putting it at the beginning and then at the high points of his Gospel. It is the voice of God himself that says to Jesus at his baptism: "Thou art my beloved Son" (v. 11), and he again designates him as his Son in the "glorious" episode of the transfiguration on the mountain (ch. 9:7). At the end it is the centurion, speaking for all the heathen, who, before the cross where Jesus has just died for the salvation of the heathen, cries out: "Truly this man was the Son of God" (ch. 15:39).

But alongside this title "Son of God" given to Jesus, the Second Gospel presents Jesus as claiming for himself the title "Son of man," and on the other hand reticent to accept the title "Messiah" (or "Christ," Greek equivalent of the Hebrew word meaning "anointed").

Two questions must be answered here. The first is to ascertain whether Jesus really claimed the title "Son of

man " or whether it was only bestowed upon him by the
early Christian community, and the second is to discover
the meaning of the title. Its application to Jesus is not at
all common in early Christianity. We find it in Mark and
the other Gospels only when it is Jesus speaking, never
when someone else is speaking to Jesus. The Evangelists
themselves never give him this name either. They therefore kept the precise memory that Jesus spoke of himself
as Son of man. But is it a Messianic title? In other words,
is it a title that official Judaism gave to the awaited Messiah? No, except in certain esoteric Jewish circles nursing
apocalyptic ideas. Jesus therefore takes up a seldom-used
expression and gives it a new meaning by combining it
with the notion of the " Suffering Servant of Yahweh "
(Isa., ch. 53). The Son of man, coming at the end of time
in the clouds of heaven (Dan. 7:13), is first of all a representative of all humanity whose function is neither war-
like nor triumphant but humble. He takes the road of the
cross to attain glory and save all men.

This established, we can understand why Jesus, according to Mark, observes the greatest silence concerning his
Messianic role and demands the same silence from others.
Thus, he enjoins the cast-out demons to be quiet (Mark
1:34; 3:12), those he has made well (chs. 1:44; 7:36;
8:26), resurrected, and those who are near them (ch.
5:43), and his very own disciples to say nothing to anyone (chs. 8:30; 9:9). The mention of this *Messianic secret* of Jesus, characteristic of the Second Gospel, is not
necessarily an invention of the Evangelist as has been asserted (Wrede), but could perfectly well be an exact
recollection to which Mark gave special importance. In
fact, this secret can be explained by the concern Jesus
had to stop any Messianic proclamation susceptible of
favoring a false interpretation of his mission. Jesus

well understood himself to be the Messiah, but he did not want to be a political Messiah, taking into his own hands the national destiny and liberating the people of Israel from the Roman occupation, the Messiah whom the average Jew was expecting.

The Second Gospel is therefore concentrated less on his teaching than on Jesus as a person, mysterious Son of man in whom faith, little by little, discovers the saving power of the Son of God.

IV. THE GOSPEL ACCORDING TO LUKE

In the Third Gospel we have before us the literary work of a chronicler. Of course, it is a real Gospel, that is, a work born of the faith of a community and founded on a tradition, rather than an individual work; but the literary personality of the author stands out much more in this Gospel than in the others.

In the prologue itself the author explains his method: "Inasmuch as many have undertaken to compile a narrative of the things which have been accomplished among us, just as they were delivered to us by those who from the beginning were eyewitnesses and ministers of the word, it seemed good to me also, having followed all things closely for some time past, to write an orderly account for you, most excellent Theophilus, that you may know the truth concerning the things of which you have been informed." (Luke 1:1-3.)

This way of taking up the matter at hand indicates, then, that the author used three sources: on the one hand, several narratives compiled before his (doubtlessly the entire Gospel of Mark); on the other hand, information acquired from eyewitnesses (and by this he implies that he was not an eyewitness himself); finally, the oral tradition of the apostles' preaching.

1. *Luke and his milieu.* Although the text of the Third Gospel does not tell us the name of its author, it enables us nevertheless to describe his personality. The first three verses already give us a glimpse of a methodical intellectual, concerned with history. The language he uses is relatively pure, and, instead of the barbarisms and neologisms of the other Evangelists, he chooses his terms from classical Greek; the author, therefore, has a regard for literature.

A comparison of his Gospel with the first two shows that he is a Gentile Christian, that is, a Christian converted from paganism. That is why he omits the most Judaic verses of Mark (such as Mark 7:27) and emphasizes, on the contrary, the words of Jesus against the Jews' unbelief and his good relations with the Samaritans, a people detested by the Jews (Luke 9:51-56; the parable of the good Samaritan in ch. 10:25-37; and ch. 17:11 ff.).

The work is dedicated to "most excellent Theophilus," who is completely unknown to us, but to whom the book of The Acts of the Apostles is also dedicated: "In the first book, O Theophilus, I have dealt with all that Jesus began to do and teach" (Acts 1:1). This "first book" can be no other than the Third Gospel, which is borne out by a philological comparison of the two works. Now, the book of The Acts is written partly in the first person plural by a travel companion of Paul. In another respect, the Third Gospel, from the second century on, is attributed to one Luke. We know of a Luke who was a companion of Paul. He is spoken of in Philemon 24: "Luke, . . . my fellow worker"; in Col. 4:14: "Luke the beloved physician . . . greets you"; and in II Tim. 4:11: "Luke alone is with me." It is not possible to invalidate or to confirm this tradition by the language or the style of the Gospel. It is true that the English critic Hobart, in 1880, tried to find in the vocabulary of the third Evangelist a confirmation of his identity with the physician Luke; he showed that medical terms were frequent: Luke 4:38; 5:18, 31; 7:10; 13:11; 22:44. But this same medical knowledge can be found in any cultured writer such as Josephus or Plutarch.

The ideas developed in The Gospel According to Luke betoken a special interest for the heathen; this, in any case, is in agreement with the attribution of this work to a companion of the apostle Paul. To be sure, the general theological orientation, especially the role attributed the death of Christ, is not the same as in the Pauline epistles, but, on the other hand, an undeniable relationship exists between Paul's writings and this Gospel, particularly in their common insistence on the role of the Holy Spirit, by which the last days are already fulfilled.

We therefore have no valid reason for doubting that the Gentile Christian author is identical with Luke, Paul's companion.

Criticism has also shown that he used the Gospel of Mark, and that he was approximately contemporaneous with Matthew. The writing of the Third Gospel is therefore situated ten or twenty years after the death of the apostle Paul, that is, about 80. As to the place where the work was composed, we can only venture to assert that the Christian community where this Gospel was born was of pagan origin — in other words, it was not Jewish. The solution for these problems must agree with that given for The Acts of the Apostles.

2. *The message of Luke.* More than in Mark or Matthew, we find in Luke the prospect of a "history of salvation." The life of Jesus is part of a greater whole, and

we are situated in the central period of a history that includes other periods, in particular that of The Acts of
the Apostles.[10] Luke looks back on Jesus' life in retro-
spect, not only as a historian who wants to recount past
events in their chronological order, but also as a believer
who knows that Christ's resurrection gives real meaning
to all that precedes. It is in the light of Easter that he re-
reads the life of Jesus; thus he designates Jesus by the title given to him by the Christian community: "Lord" (in
Greek, *Kyrios*).

The title "Lord" expresses better than any other the
fact that Christ has been lifted up to the right hand of
God and that as the Glorified One he is presently interceding in man's behalf. When the early Christians gave
Jesus the title of *Kyrios,* they were thereby proclaiming
that he did not belong only to the past in the history of
salvation, that he is not only the object of a future expectation, but that he is also a present, living reality, that
he can enter into contact with us, that the believer can
address his prayers to him, and that the church can in-
voke him in worship so that he will offer her prayers to
God and make them effectual. One of the first Christian
confessions of faith could be kept to two words: "*Kyrios
Iēsous,*" Jesus is Lord.

Of course the word "Lord" is found in the other Gospels, with the meaning of a polite Semitic title, as equivalent to our "Sir," or, with even more respect, "My
Lord"; but Luke is the only Evangelist who uses this
term absolutely: "the Lord" (chs. 7:13; 10:1, 39, 41;
11:39; 12:42; 13:15; 17:5; 18:6; 19:8; 22:61; 24:3, 34).

[10] This outline is already one proof that the author of the Third
Gospel is the same as the author of The Acts of the Apostles.
Hans Conzelmann has spoken of "periodization" (*Die Mitte
der Zeit,* 1962).

When he speaks of the Kingdom of God, Luke has especially in mind, in this respect different from Matthew, the future Kingdom yet to be seen (ch. 9:27) and which must be believed in, rather than the mysterious active presence of this Kingdom. For Luke, the existing, dynamic presence of God is less the Kingdom than the *Holy Spirit.* John the Baptist, his mother, and his father are filled with the Holy Spirit (ch. 1:15, 41, 67) as well as old Simeon (ch. 2:25-27). Jesus possesses the power of the Spirit; he exults in the Spirit (chs. 4:1, 14, 18; 10:21). It is the Spirit that is to give to the disciples what they are to say when persecuted (ch. 12:12). Therefore, they must ask for the Spirit in prayer: "If you then, who are evil, know how to give good gifts to your children, how much more will the heavenly Father give the Holy Spirit [Matthew says here, " good things," Matt. 7:11] to those who ask him " (Luke 11:13). And we find instead of the request in the Lord's Prayer, " Thy kingdom [or " thy reign "] come," a variant attested by a few sources: " May thy Holy Spirit come upon us, and may he sanctify us " (v. 2).

We have already pointed out that Luke readily omits the more " Jewish " traditions concerning Jesus and his teachings, traditions that are given by the other Evangelists. The positive counterpart of these voluntary omissions is Luke's insistence on the *universalism of the gospel.* Luke's genealogy of Jesus goes back beyond Abraham (cf. Matthew) to Adam, the first man (ch. 3:38). On Christmas night the angels sing: " Peace on men whom God loves " (ch. 2:14). Jesus is the salvation and the light of all the peoples (vs. 31-32), and he sends his preaching of pardon to all nations (ch. 24:47). The Gospel of Luke is also the *gospel of the poor.* Jesus' solicitude is especially for the poor — sinners of both sexes,

publicans, widows and little children, robbers and re-
pentant ones, sick men and women. The poor, in the real
sense of those who lack material well-being, are called
blessed (ch. 6:20), and the rich are called, not bad, but
woeful (ch. 6:24). The good news (the gospel) is for the
poor (chs. 4:18; 7:22), and that is Luke's purpose in
sketching in ethical principles throughout ch. 16.

Finally, we will emphasize the atmosphere of joyous
praise that resounds in this Gospel. The purest praise appears in the hymns that the universal Christian church
has adopted in its worship to sing the praises of Jesus
Christ, the Lord: Mary's hymn (the Magnificat, ch. 1:46-
55), Zechariah's (Benedictus, vs. 68-79), that of the angels of Bethlehem (Gloria in Excelsis, ch. 2:14), and that
of the old man Simeon (the Nunc Dimittis, ch. 2:29-32).
Such is the joy of the Evangelist who knows that he, with
the community, has been made a part of a history in
which the life of Jesus is the center.

V. THE GOSPEL ACCORDING TO JOHN

1. *The Fourth Gospel and the Synoptics.* We have mentioned that the Fourth Gospel is different from the others. However, we cannot isolate it entirely from the Synoptics because it *presupposes* that they are known, or at
least the tradition which they relate. For example, in
John 1:40, Andrew is introduced to us as the brother of
Simon Peter, whereas Simon Peter has not as yet been
mentioned. At a few points, we have the impression that
this Gospel is trying to rectify the data given by the Synoptics, as though its information were more reliable than
theirs: In ch. 3:24, it is stated that " John [the Baptist]
had not yet been put in prison " when Jesus had already
begun his ministry; according to Mark, on the contrary,

Jesus began preaching only after the imprisonment of John the Baptist (Mark 1:14).

Elsewhere, the Johannine writings differ from the Synoptics, not only in the chronological and geographical setting given for the narrative of Jesus' life, but also in *different theological viewpoints.*

It goes over the same events as the Synoptics, but from a distance. It is rather a profound meditation on the central events of the history of salvation. Its purpose is to show forth the identity between the historical Jesus and the Christ who is present in his church, to trace lines going from every event in Jesus' life to every manifestation of the life of Jesus Christ, glorified Lord, in the church. The subject matter of this Gospel is not, therefore, as some have claimed, abstract truth, but a whole collection of historical events, presented as the high point of all divine revelation. Far from denying the biography of Jesus, in a historical mysticism, the Evangelist takes it very seriously. The events need to be real to be meaningful; they are not symbols but realities, but their bearing goes far beyond the instant of their happening and reaches out to the whole history of salvation.

Jesus Christ, in this Gospel, is both human and divine, and far from being a Docetist, the author combats "Docetism" itself (a doctrine according to which Jesus had only the appearance of a man): Jesus Christ is the "*logos,*" the preexistent Word of God, but he is the incarnated "*logos,*" the Word made flesh (John 1:14). In his conclusion, the Evangelist himself indicates the purpose of his work: "These are written that you may believe that Jesus is the Christ, the Son of God, and that believing you may have life in his name" (ch. 20:31).

2. *Historical worth of the Fourth Gospel.* The well-defined theological viewpoint directs the choice of the

narratives and *logia* recounted, as well as the way in which they are put into writing. Thus the author often lengthens the lines and makes the historical Jesus say what the Holy Spirit has revealed to the author himself. In another respect, this viewpoint led him to mix, with a certain lack of historical concern, the exposition of the consequences of Jesus' life for the era of the church with that of the life of Jesus itself. That is why many critics would prefer to consider this Gospel to be a document completely lacking in historical worth; whereas, in spite of the historical liberties taken because of its special viewpoint, it is a valid source of information for the facts, and even, in a few points at least, more certain than the Synoptics. For example, the Synoptics consider that the fifteenth of Nisan, the day of the Jewish Passover feast, is the day of Jesus' death. The last meal that Jesus took with his disciples and during which he instituted the " Lord's Supper " took place, according to them, the evening before, and would therefore have been the Jewish Passover meal. Now, according to the Fourth Gospel, Jesus was crucified on the fourteenth of Nisan, the morning of the day on which the Jews ate the Passover lamb. Jesus' last meal with his disciples, therefore, took place on the thirteenth of Nisan and could not be considered to be a Passover meal. Should we not here give preference to the Fourth Gospel? For it is difficult to imagine that the assembly of the Sanhedrin and all the Jews' proceedings before the crucifixion could have taken place on the great feast day of the fifteenth of Nisan.[11] Moreover, certain details of the Synoptics themselves are not in agreement

[11] If the date given by the Synoptics is combined with that of the Johannine Gospel by bringing in the calendar difference of the Qumran sect (A. Jaubert), the chronological indication of the Fourth Gospel still retains its historical worth.

with their own chronological context. According to Mark 15:21, and Luke 23:26, Simon of Cyrene, " who was coming in from the field," was forced to carry Jesus' cross. If, as is probable if not certain, this means that he had been working in the fields, it is incompatible with the absolute prohibition for the Jews to work on Passover Day, the fifteenth of Nisan; whereas the possibility is perfectly reasonable for the fourteenth of Nisan.

Generally speaking, the chronological setting of the Johannine Gospel, more extended than that of the Synoptics, could also be more exact. Tradition always has a way of concentrating events, and the two or three years of the Fourth Gospel are more realistic than the single year given by the Synoptics for Jesus' ministry. Here again, the Synoptics themselves carry indications of the perhaps artificially restrained nature of their chronological and geographical setting. Thus, while they have Jesus go up to Jerusalem only once, they suppose that he had friends there when he arrived (cf. Matt. 21:17; Mark 11:11, 19; 14:3), and when Jesus cries out (according to Matthew), " Jerusalem, Jerusalem, . . . how often would I have gathered your children together! " (Matt. 23:37), this exclamation does not fit in very well with a single journey.

3. *Date of composition and milieu of origin.* If the Fourth Gospel presupposes the Synoptic Gospels, it is posterior to them. Ignatius, Bishop of Antioch, who died a martyr's death in 107 or 112, seems to have referred to it without quoting it directly. A rather late date is usually ascribed to the writing of this Gospel (Albert Schweitzer even places it in the second century after Ignatius of Antioch). In 1935, a papyrus was discovered containing a fragment of the Johannine Gospel (John 18:31-33), which the papyrologists dated from the be-

ginning of the second century, perhaps even from the end of the first. Unless this fragment is part of an earlier tradition, used *both* by this papyrus and our Gospel, it is no longer possible to admit any period after the years 90 to 95 for the composition of the Fourth Gospel.

The tradition that is based on the testimony of Irenaeus claims that the Johannine Gospel is of Ephesian origin; other indications lead us, rather, to seek its origin in Antioch. Its style and its language (Aramaicisms) carry the mark of a double influence, Hellenistic and Judaic, and it is not necessary to choose, as is usually done, between these two influences as though they were mutually exclusive, representing two totally different milieu. Alongside of the official Judaism of Palestine (Sadducees and Pharisees), another type of Judaism must not be forgotten — the esoteric Judaism, the existence of which has been attested in Palestine and Syria. In it we find a particular current of thought, the importance of which has been clearly shown by the documents discovered at Qumran. These Jews, more or less related to the Essenes, attributed a primary role to knowledge, to all kinds of baptisms, and used a vocabulary which brings to mind that of Hellenistic syncretism (André Dupont-Sommer). To the two currents of Palestinian Judaism (official Judaism and nonconformist Judaism), there probably corresponded, although they had undergone profound transformations, two analogous currents within early Christianity in Palestine. The Synoptics would represent the first current, and the Fourth Gospel the second, which possibly included also the " Hellenists " in Palestine mentioned in the book of The Acts of the Apostles (Acts, chs. 6 to 8; 11:19-20). The intermixing of Semitic and Greek thought in the Fourth Gospel is easily explained if the author came, as we believe, from this Hellenistic branch of Palestinian Judaism.

4. *The main Johannine ideas.* We have already defined the particular theological viewpoint of this Gospel: the author endeavors to draw a connecting line between the historical Jesus and the Christ of the church with the intention of showing their identity.

It is this intention which leads him to see with a single eye certain events from Jesus' life and some of the realities of the life of the church, its mission (John 4:31 ff.; 12:20 ff.), and its worship "in spirit and in truth," in which the divine glory is no longer connected with the temple but with the person of the dead and resurrected Christ (chs. 1:14, 51; 2:13 ff.; 4:19 ff.). Thus the miracle at Cana (ch. 2:1-12) and the feeding of the five thousand (ch. 6:1-13) prefigure the Sacrament of the Lord's Supper (Eucharist), just as the healing of the lame man at Bethesda (ch. 5:1-14) and that of the blind man from birth (ch. 9:1-7) announce Baptism, and the water and the blood coming from Jesus' side after his death (ch. 19:34) unite in one single fact a reference to these two Sacraments. The sermon on the "bread of life" (ch. 6:22-59) also is a veritable doctrinal exposition on the Eucharist, and the discussion with Nicodemus (ch. 3:1-21) an authentic baptismal catechism.

The continuity between Jesus incarnate and Christ present in his church appears especially in the promise of the Holy Spirit, designated in the "farewell talks" (chs. 14 to 17) by the term "Paraclete" (comforter, advocate). He is to enable the disciples to understand the meaning of Jesus' life and words as the Evangelist depicts him in his work. He is to lead them into all truth; but, on the other hand, Christ himself is the truth and the word, just as he is light, life, and resurrection (ch. 11:25). Here, the topic of life takes the place belonging to the topic of the Kingdom in the Synoptics. Life is both a divine benefit hoped for at the end of time and a benefit now present in Christ's person.

Johannine eschatology (the doctrine dealing with the end of time) is also particular: no description of the end of the world or of Christ's return for the Last Judgment. Christ's glory has already been manifested, chs. 1:14; 2:11; 11:4, 40); salvation has already been obtained (ch. 5:24); the world has already been judged (ch. 3:18-19); and the prince of this world already cast out (chs. 12:31; 16:33). In Christ's death the apex of world history has been attained. Therefore, eschatology has already been accomplished.

However, the Fourth Gospel knows what the tension is between the "already" and the "not yet" found throughout the New Testament, but it has its own way of emphasizing the "already." Even so, its message is not timeless, and it clearly admits an end to man's history, since it frequently refers to the resurrection of the dead at the Last Day (chs. 5:28; 6:39, 40, 44, 54). However, here again the emphasis is put on the anticipated fulfillment of this announcement, for Jesus himself is the resurrection and the life (ch. 11:23-26). History, as it stretches back into the past or forward into the future, is concentrated in his being.

Finally, the Fourth Gospel is the *gospel of love* — God loved the world (ch. 3:16); he loves Christ (chs. 3:35; 15:9); Christ loves his own to the point of dying for them (ch. 13:1); and Christians, after his death, are to effect their union with him by loving one another (v. 34).

5. *The author of the Fourth Gospel.* The classical tradition according to which the author of this Gospel is John, son of Zebedee, one of the twelve apostles, is not attested earlier than the testimony of Irenaeus who wrote

only at the end of the second century: "John, the disciple of the Lord, wrote the Gospel when he was in Ephesus in Asia."

What would give weight to the testimony of Irenaeus is the fact that, before he was Bishop of Lyons, he knew Polycarp, Bishop of Smyrna, and Polycarp, according to Irenaeus, often recalled his former relationship "with John and the others who had seen the Lord" (letter of Irenaeus to Florinus).

Another tradition, based on vague expressions from the pen of Papias (Bishop of Hierapolis, earlier than Irenaeus, known to us only by what the ecclesiastical historian Eusebius has to say about him), sometimes speaks of John the apostle, sometimes of John the elder. That is why some critics have attributed the Fourth Gospel to John the elder, who is then other than the son of Zebedee.

As early as the end of the second century, the authenticity of the Johannine authorship of the Fourth Gospel was called in question. True, this was motivated by doctrinal struggles, and therefore the motivations were scientifically questionable.

But real difficulties crop up when, after these "external" testimonies of ancient writers who give us no sure information, we interrogate the Gospel itself (of course, the title, "The Gospel According to John" was not given to it until long after its first writing and was not included in the original) concerning whether or not its author is the apostle John, son of Zebedee. This identification is never explicitly stated, and, without being absolutely excluded, is not even suggested by the text. The Evangelist only claims to be an eyewitness, if we accept as such the use of the first person plural in ch. 1:14, and especially the "signature" of ch. 19:35: "He who saw it has borne witness — his testimony is true, and he knows that he tells the truth — that you also may believe " (cf. also chs. 20:30-31 and 21:24-25). Elsewhere, the Gospel twice mentions (chs. 1:35-40 and 18:15) the presence of an anonymous disciple who could easily be the author. Finally, and especially, a disciple is mentioned several times " whom Jesus loved " (chs. 13:23; 19:26; 20:2; 21:7, 20). This " beloved " disciple is described as an eyewitness and is always anonymous — could he be the author?

Two modern critics, Alfred Loisy and Maurice Goguel, have maintained that this beloved disciple was not historical but an ideal, that of the perfect disciple. This theory is contrary to the connection between history and theology in the Johannine Gospel (see above, pp. 45 and 49). Even more, according to ch. 21:22-23, the tradition was widespread that the beloved disciple was not to die; when ch. 21 was written, the error of this tradition is recognized (cf. v. 23), doubtlessly because it was acknowledged that the beloved disciple was quite dead, which would hardly be suitable for an ideal. Lastly, the comparison of the beloved disciple with Peter who could not be an ideal renders this theory untenable.

Chapter 21 does not seem to have come from the same author as chs. 1 to 20 (ch. 20:30-31 is clearly a conclusion), but rather by one of the Evangelist's disciples, or, more correctly, by a group of disciples (in ch. 21:24 we find the first person plural). Chapters 1 to 20 would, in that case, have been written toward the end of their author's life, who would be the beloved disciple. Chapter 21 was added afterward, partly to explain his death, by a disciple who lightly retouched the body of the Gospel as well.

But can the beloved disciple be identified with someone mentioned in the Gospel? Chapter 21:2 clearly takes notice of the anonymity of the sons of Zebedee. We would, on the other hand, be tempted to propose a rather fascinating hypothesis, although it is not sustained by indisputable arguments: the beloved disciple = Lazarus who was raised from the dead. Here are the factors that can be brought up in favor of this hypothesis: (1) The fourth Gospel is the only one that mentions Lazarus, and it places him among Jesus' close companions. It is also the only one that mentions a beloved disciple who, although he is one of Jesus' intimate friends, is not necessarily part of the group of twelve apostles. (2) Lazarus is the only person of whom it is also said that Jesus loved him (cf. ch. 11:3, 5, 35-36). (3) When ch. 21 informs us of the rumor going around that the beloved disciple would not die, might we not think of Lazarus whom Jesus had resurrected from the dead?

But it must not be forgotten that this identification is entirely hypothetical. We must resign ourselves to not knowing with certainty the name of the beloved disciple. However, we can say this about him:

a. He comes from a different theological world than that of the other Evangelists, perhaps from the Hellenists of Palestine or Syria (see above, pp. 48 f.);

b. He is not necessarily part of the group of the Twelve who, as such, do not have any role in this Gospel, whereas it mentions other intimate disciples of Jesus;

c. He does not seem to belong to the same social milieu as the other disciples of Jesus (he was an acquaintance of the High Priest, cf. ch. 18:15-16);

d. He is perhaps from Jerusalem (historically he is well-informed concerning Jerusalem traditions).

VI. The Acts of the Apostles

1. *Title and contents.* The contents of the book do not correspond to its title, because not all the apostles are included, only Peter and Paul (John only appears briefly). On the other hand it is not the " acts " of these apostles which are found in this book, but rather the story of the spreading of the gospel from Jerusalem to Rome by the action of the Holy Spirit.

By its purpose as well as by its literary form, this book is not different from the Gospels. It is still a *euangelion*. Moreover, the Gospel of Luke and The Acts of the Apostles (as we have already seen while studying the Gospel of Luke) formed two volumes of the same work. Perhaps this work was divided only later on by the insertion of the Fourth Gospel (Menoud).

The purpose of the second volume is to show the powerful action of the Holy Spirit in the first Christian community, and from it, to the surrounding world. This purpose determines the choice of historical material — the author did not retain what was contrary to his subject or that which, from this point of view, did not interest him.

It is in this light that the abrupt ending to the " story " of Peter must be explained (" Then he departed and went to another place," Acts 12:17) [12] as well as that of the " story " of Paul (ch. 28:30-31). It is also the source of gaps and deformations. The speeches of Peter, Stephen, and Paul, while they retain the major ideas of each person, reflect the personal theology of the author (Wilckens, Haenchen). Many facts recounted by the book of The Acts are found in Paul's epistles, sometimes with differences of telling that lead one to believe that the author

[12] His reappearance in Acts, ch. 15, is only momentary.

of The Acts was not acquainted with the Pauline epistles. Thus, when a comparison is made of Acts 15:1-29 and Gal. 2:1-10, which very probably deal with the same event, the Jerusalem " conference," a meeting of the apostles who had come to Jerusalem to compare their experiences and problems in missionary work, clear differences can be discerned. According to Gal., ch. 2, the apostolic conference decides that henceforth the Jewish and heathen missions be separated (ch. 2:7-9), whereas, according to Acts, ch. 15, the result of the conference is a decree enjoining Christians of heathen origin to submit to certain regulations of the Jewish law (ch. 15:23-29).

The book of The Acts, by its stories of conversions (chs. 9:1-20; 16:13-15, 24-34), of healings (chs. 3:1-11; 9:33-35; 14:8-10), its vivid portraits of the life of the early Christian church (chs. 2:42 ff.; 4:32 ff.; 5:11), the theological speeches attributed to Peter (chs. 2:14-36; 3:12-26; 11:5-17), Stephen (ch. 7:2-53), and Paul (chs. 13:16-41; 17:22-31; 22:1-21), constitutes also an *apology* for Christianity.

2. *Author, date, and sources.* We have seen that the author is the same as for The Gospel According to Luke, for he refers to a first volume dedicated to the same Theophilus. The vocabulary, language, style, and theological ideas are the same. As in the Gospel (Luke 1:10), the author utilized sources the traces of which can easily be found, especially in the first part which describes the life of the early community.

Among the documents that he may have used as sources for the second part, many exegetes have thought that he had a " diary," a travel diary transcribed word for word in several passages. In fact, in Acts, ch. 16, the narrative changes abruptly over from the third person plural, " They went down to Troas; and a vision appeared to Paul in the night . . ." (ch. 16:8-9), to the first person plural, " And when he had seen the vision, immediately *we* sought to go on into Macedonia . . ." (v. 10).[13] After this the text includes long portions written with " we," which would be perfectly well explained if the author in these spots were using passages from the travel diary of one of Paul's companions in apostleship.

The question that comes up now is whether the authors of the entire book and of the part with " we " are identical or if the first recopied some pages from the second's diary. Antiquity gives us examples of texts in which the first and third persons alternate. We can therefore suppose that the author utilized, for the second part, the diary of a group of Paul's companions, and, especially for the passages with " we," his own diary (Trocmé).

Let us admit, then, that the author of The Acts is Luke, Paul's companion and author of the Third Gospel. In that case, since the book of The Acts is the follow-up of the Gospel of Luke and the latter dates from about 80, the book of The Acts was probably written between 80 and 90.

13 According to the Codex Bezae, the text of The Acts changes over to the first person plural in ch. 11:28.

Chapter 5

The Pauline Corpus

PAULINE CHRONOLOGY

The problem of the date of each of the Pauline epistles is easier to solve than for most ancient documents. Thus, in our study of the Pauline Corpus (that is, of the canonical collection of the letters traditionally attributed to the apostle Paul), we will follow the chronological order and not that of the canon in which the epistles are arranged according to length.

A difference must be made between relative chronology and absolute chronology.

The relative chronology of Paul's life can be established according to the data given by The Epistle to the Galatians, complemented by The Acts of the Apostles. We then have the following rough sketch:

a. From the conversion of Paul on the road to Damascus to his first visit to the apostles at Jerusalem, three years passed;

b. Paul's first missionary journey, followed by a second visit to Jerusalem, lasted thirteen or fourteen years;

c. Paul's second and third missionary journeys, followed by his arrest at Jerusalem, make up a period of six and one half years;

    d. Paul is in prison at Caesarea for two years;

    e. The prisoner is taken to Rome; the trip lasts one year;

    f. Paul is prisoner at Rome for two years.

One established point in this relative chronology, then, is enough to obtain the absolute chronology. Ancient chronology can give us this landmark.

The date in Paul's history that used to be chosen to furnish this landmark was the recalling to Rome of the procurator before whom Paul had to defend himself, Antonius Felix, and his replacement by Porcius Festus. This succession is mentioned in Acts 24:27, when Paul, prisoner at Caesarea, was about to appear before Porcius Festus. Now, three documents, a passage from the *Annales* of Tacitus, and a text each from Josephus and Eusebius, give the length of the functions of Felix and Festus. Unfortunately, the texts are neither clear nor unanimous, and we can only conclude that Festus replaced Felix in 60, in 56, or in 59.

Today we have a more certain landmark. In Acts 18:12-17, concerning Paul's sojourn in Corinth, the proconsul Gallio is mentioned. The date of Gallio's proconsulate in Achaia is known to us by an inscription found at Delphi and published by Bourguet. This inscription is a copy of a letter from the emperor Claudius to the inhabitants of Delphi and gives us the incidental news that Gallio was proconsul of Achaia during the twenty-sixth acclamation of the emperor, in 51 or 52.

According to Acts 18:11, Paul stayed in Corinth for one year and six months when Gallio was proconsul, then left for Ephesus, then for Jerusalem, etc. Festus therefore replaced Felix in 57 and Paul was converted in 32.

As a result, if we can arrange the Pauline epistles according to the events of Paul's life, we will be able to date them. This is how we know that the first epistle to the Thessalonians was written in the year 50 and that it is the earliest Christian writing we have.

I. THE FIRST EPISTLES

1. *The First Epistle to the Thessalonians.* Thessalonica was founded around 300 B.C. by Cassander of Macedonia in honor of his wife Thessalonica. This city (which was later called Salonika) was an important meeting place for East and West, and when this epistle was written, the Roman proconsul resided there. According to the historian Strabo, it was a thickly populated city, and inscriptions show that many Jews lived there.

It is during his second missionary journey that Paul arrives in Thessalonica, accompanied by Silas and Timothy (Acts 17:1-15). They preach in the city synagogue and there convert several Jews and especially heathen who have accepted Judaism without submitting to its ritual laws; but these conversions arouse the jealousy of the other Jews who provoke a riot, and Paul and Silas are forced to flee the city at night and take refuge at Berea.

This historical data from the book of The Acts is confirmed by the first epistle to the Thessalonians. We learn there that Paul has sent his disciple Timothy from Athens (I Thess. 3:1) to obtain information concerning the community of Thessalonica (vs. 2-5), and that Timothy has brought back to Paul not only good news (v. 6) but a series of doctrinal questions on eschatology that have been bothering the members of this church. Meantime, Paul has probably gone to Corinth. After his departure, discussion has arisen regarding the fate of those Christians who die before Christ's return (ch. 4:13 ff.) and regarding the date of this return (ch. 5:1 ff.). Paul answers these questions, and the teaching which he dispenses, based on one of Jesus' statements, decides the main theological interest of this epistle — those who will be living at the time of Christ's last coming will have no advantage over the dead, for the latter will be resurrected when the last trumpet sounds.

We have seen that this epistle was most probably written in 50. Its authenticity was questioned in the nineteenth century by the Hegelians of the theological school of Tübingen. According to them, ch. 2:16, " But God's wrath has come upon them [the Jews] at last! " is an allusion to the destruction of Jerusalem in 70. This epistle would therefore have been written after Paul's death. But there is a positive argument in favor of authenticity. The fact that eschatological problems, which presuppose the expectation of an imminent end, are being discussed in Thessalonica indicates a situation that corresponds to the earliest period of the church, when the first Christians, and Paul himself (at least at the beginning of his apostolic ministry) were expecting Christ's return for their generation.

Another indication tells in favor of the Pauline authenticity of this epistle — the heads of the Thessalonian church are designated by the term *proistamenoi*, " leaders " (ch. 5:12), which is to disappear very rapidly to be replaced by the term *episkopoi*, " overseers." We are therefore at an early level of the organizational development of the Christian communities.

2. *The Second Epistle to the Thessalonians.* The second epistle to the Thessalonians contains fewer direct allusions to the historical situation than does the first.

Where was the apostle when he wrote this second letter? We are not able to infer this either from the letter itself or from the book of The Acts. However, the situation must not be too different from what it was when the first epistle was written. Timothy and Silas are still with Paul (II Thess. 1:1), and the Thessalonian church is still debating eschatology (ch. 2:1 ff.). The supposition is made, then, that Paul wrote this second epistle shortly after the first, that he was still at Corinth (cf. Acts, ch. 18), and that he had received news from the Thessalonians since the last letter. Therefore, here again it is the year 50.

The Pauline authenticity of this second epistle is contested by many critics, even by some who accept that of the first. The historical allusions, for them, are only literary fiction. Here are the critics' two principal arguments:

a. The theological content of the two epistles is contradictory. The end, according to the first, will appear suddenly; according to the second, only after a certain number of events;

b. Repetitions of the first epistle are found in the second. For example, II Thess. 2:13-17 is an approximate reproduction of I Thess. 3:7-13.

The following hypothesis is then constructed: A Christian, after Paul's death, disapproved of I Thessalonians and tried to replace it by another epistle of his own making (II Thessalonians) by more or less directly recopying passages from I Thessalonians to deceive the reader.

What is the answer to these arguments?

a. The main idea of each of these epistles and especially their ideas concerning the end are not contradictory but rather complementary. Jewish apocalyptic literature also unites them.

b. As for the repetitions, they can be explained while admitting the identity of the authors: Paul must write a lot, and he repeated himself, or else, seeing that his first letter left room for misunderstanding, he wrote a second, taking up the same ideas with other words to correct the misunderstandings.

Although literary property did not exist at that time, would it not be necessary, in the case of this epistle, if the writer were other than Paul, to ascribe to him a cynical purpose of deceiving his readers? For we read in II Thess. 2:1-2: "We beg you, brethren, not to be quickly shaken in mind . . . by letter purporting to be from us," and in ch. 3:17: "I, Paul, write this greeting with my own hand. This is the mark in every letter of mine; it is the way I write." If, as we believe, these verses are from Paul's hand, they prove two things: first, that Paul had the habit of using a secretary (Silvanus or Timothy of ch. 1:1?), and next, that already during Paul's lifetime letters existed which were falsely attributed to him.

Already in his first epistle, Paul had put them on their guard against the "inspiration" of the Holy Spirit without controls. There were doubtless a great many illuminated ones at Thessalonica, and this illuminism was connected with a feverish expectation of Christ's coming. The apostle had written that they were always to be ready for this event, but he wanted also to turn the Thessalonians away from date calculations concerning this return which was to come as "a thief in the night." He was not understood. The recipients thought that Christ's return was imminent, that all that was left for them to do was to stop all work and anxiously wait. Paul, in his second letter, puts things right: premonitory events will announce the great day (ch. 2:3); there is one thing (a person) in particular which is "holding back" the end; they must stay calm and keep on working (ch. 3:6-12). To show that he is not contradicting himself, the apostle recalls that what he is now writing is in conformity with what he taught them in person when he was in Thessalonica (ch. 2:5) and with what he wrote in his first letter (ch. 2:15) from which, moreover, he takes a good many ideas (II Thess. 2:13-17 similar to I Thess. 3:7-13).

II. THE GREAT EPISTLES

The Pauline authenticity of the four epistles with which we are now going to deal has never, a few exceptions aside, been questioned. They are the masterworks of the apostle Paul's thought and offer great theological interest.

1. *The Epistle to the Galatians.* Doctrinally [14] this epistle has played a particular role in the periods of combat in church history, during the Reformation of the sixteenth century, for example.

The foremost subject, dealing with the relationship between law and grace, works and faith in the redemptive act of Jesus Christ, will be met again, more comprehensively and methodically developed, in the epistle to the Romans that we will study below. Here, Paul's thought is still at the stage of elaboration. Besides, the occasion that prompts this epistle is different. It is born of an attack directed against Paul himself, against his teaching and his apostolic authority, by Judaizing Christians who are still attached to the law and have not understood the newness of the gospel (cf. Gal. 1:6 to 3:1). Paul insists on the fact that he received the gospel directly by a revelation from Christ, and, without the intermediary of human transmission, he also received apostleship, a unique function excluding any man-to-man transmission.

Let us try to define the historical situation and the date

[14] Paul gives information about his life in this epistle, with a theological purpose, which is very useful to us; cf. Gal. 1:13 to 2:14.

of the epistle to the Galatians.

Who are the Galatians? The question is not so simple as it may seem, for two countries in Asia Minor, one in the north, the other to the south, were named Galatia.

Northern Galatia, the region of Pessinus and Ancyra (modern Ankara), between Pontus, Bithynia, and Lycaonia, was inhabited by a Celtic population (whence the word "Galatians") who had settled there at the beginning of the third century B.C. In 50 B.C., Amyntas, the last king of the Galatians, linked Lycaonia and Pisidia, two southern regions, to his territory. At his death in 25 B.C., the entire territory ruled by Amyntas went to the Romans who made of it a single province administrated by the same legate. This Roman province, spreading from north to south, had a very long title enumerating all the regions it took in. This title, for convenience's sake, was shortened to "Galatia," as Tacitus, Ptolemy, and Pliny attest. Popular usage, however, seems to have reserved the word "Galatia" for the northern region.

Now, Paul traveled through southern Galatia (the region of Pisidia, Iconium, Lystra, and Derbe) during his first missionary journey. He founded churches there (according to Acts 13:14 ff.), which he revisited during his second journey (Acts 16:1). But he also went into northern Galatia during this second missionary journey, founded churches there also (Acts 16:6), revisiting them during his third journey (Acts 18:23).

To which of these churches, those of the north or of the south, was Paul writing? The date to be given our epistle depends on the answer to that question. It is improbable that he called "Galatians" the inhabitants of the Hellenized cities of southern Galatia (cf. Gal. 3:1: "O foolish Galatians"). Obviously a third solution is possible: Paul wrote to all the churches of the Roman province of Galatia, from north to south; but the precise, direct invectives hurled at the " Galatians " could not be proper for all the churches so different from one another. He is, therefore, addressing a small and very localized group of churches.

Again, when the book of The Acts speaks of a " region of Galatia " (Acts 16:6; 18:23), it is always in association with Phrygia, a northern region, and to mark a part of a northward journey of the apostles.

We conclude, therefore, that this epistle is addressed to Christians of Celtic extraction in northern Galatia, the region of Pessinus and Ancyra.

What is the date of its writing? In Gal. 4:13, Paul recalls that during his " first stay " with the Galatians, he had been sick. He had therefore been there twice. If northern Galatia is referred to, the two visits are not those of Acts 13:14 and 16:1 (southern Galatia), but rather those of chs. 16:6 and 18:23. This epistle was therefore written after the second of Paul's trips through northern Galatia, that is, during the third missionary journey, consequently at the earliest toward 52–53, and probably at Ephesus.

2. *The First Epistle to the Corinthians.* The problem of the addressees of this epistle does not come up, for we are well informed regarding the city and the church of Corinth.

Corinth, an opulent Greek city with two ports, destroyed in 146 B.C. by Mummius and reconstructed under Julius Caesar and Augustus, was a cosmopolitan commercial center. All the forms of worship and all the philosophies of that time came together there. It was a city where all kinds of disorder cropped up, and it had such a reputation for licentiousness and debauchery that the expression " live like a Corinthian " had gone into everyday language to designate a dissolute life.

The church of Corinth, especially made up of Christians of pagan origin and coming from modest circumstances, was founded by Paul. We find the narrative of this founding in Acts 18:1-18; this was in 51, when Gallio, whom we have already mentioned, was proconsul. Paul proclaims the gospel in the synagogue and the Jews stir up opposition. He then turns toward the heathen, but the Jews' opposition becomes violent when Crispus, ruler of the synagogue, is converted to Christianity with all his family. The proconsul Gallio, for his part, refuses to get mixed up in a Jewish quarrel. After a year and a half, Paul leaves Corinth.

The New Testament contains two epistles to the Corinthians. But Paul sent four letters to this church, two of which are now lost. Before our first epistle to the Corinthians, and thanks to it, we can situate one of them, for Paul alludes to it in I Cor. 5:9: " I wrote to you in my first letter." The other (that mentioned in II Cor. 2:4) can be situated between our two canonical epistles. The first epistle to the Corinthians is really, therefore, the second of the four and our second epistle to the Corinthians is the last.

The historical data of The Acts of the Apostles is confirmed by our first epistle to the Corinthians. According to The Acts, the Corinthian church is composed of a majority of Gentile Christians and a minority of Jewish Christians; for we read in I Cor. 12:2: " When you were heathen . . . ," and in ch. 7:18: " Was any one at the time of his call already circumcised? Let him not seek to remove the marks of circumcision."

The church includes numerous slaves (cf. ch. 7:21: " Were you a slave when called? Never mind "), but few intellectuals or rich persons: " For consider your call, brethren; not many of you were wise according to worldly standards, not many were powerful, not many were of noble birth " (ch. 1:26).

However, the epistle takes into account a certain diversity and even divisions within the community. According to ch. 1:12, there were four " parties " claiming respectively Paul, Apollos, Peter, and Christ.

The " party of Paul " was perhaps made up of the first Christians in the church, converted by Paul in 51. The " party of Apollos " was doubtless united around the teaching of Apollos, a well-educated Alexandrian Jew, member of the sect of John the Baptist before becoming a Christian, who came to Corinth (Acts 19:1) and is introduced as a good preacher, well versed in Biblical knowledge (cf. ch. 18:24-28). It is therefore a question of a party including an intellectual minority, and it is probably for the latter that the apostle gives, in the first chapter, a particularly profound teaching concerning the difference between human wisdom and the wisdom of God accessible to man only by faith in revelation and by the Holy Spirit. Did the " party of Peter " gather together the Jewish Christians from Palestine where they had been baptized by the apostle? Or had Peter come to Corinth?

As to the strange " party of Christ," it has given the exegetes much difficulty. Is it a group of sectarians claiming for themselves a monopoly on Christ's name? But the proximity of this name with Paul's, Peter's, and Apollos' is no less curious. Several hypotheses have been put forward, none of which is certain. We will give two of them, one clever, the other more likely. Some have proposed to read, instead of *Christos* in I Cor. 1:12, *Crispos*. A copyist would have made the mistake because of the graphical resemblance of the Greek words written in capitals. The party in question was formed around Crispus, the ruler of the synagogue of Corinth, converted by Paul according to Acts 18:8, and whom our epistle speaks of again, right after enumerating the four " parties," in I Cor. 1:14: " I baptized none of you except Crispus." Others have thought to understand the expression " I belong to Christ " (ch. 1:12) either as Paul's personal remark, or as an exclamation in parentheses of an early copyist of the epistle. According to this hypothesis, indignant at the Corinthian divisions, the latter wished to add in the margin his personal confession of faith: " As for me, I belong to Christ! " and the following copyist put this marginal annotation into the text, in accord with what we have said about the origin of certain variants of detail from one manuscript to another. (See above, Chapter 1.) In favor of this hypothesis we could cite several verses in ch. 3 where the internal divisions are again mentioned (ch. 3:3-7 and 21-23). The fourth party is not named (not even that of Peter in ch. 3:4) and Paul entreats the Corinthians to throw in their lot with Christ.

The apostle is writing this letter to try to reestablish unity in the Corinthian church about which he has received bad news (ch. 1:11). Besides this important subject of unity treated from chs. 1 to 4, we find in this epistle teachings on the sexual problem in chs. 5 and 6; on marriage in ch. 7; on Christian liberty and the respect due to the feeble in the " faith " in ch. 8; on the right of the minister of the gospel to live from his preaching in ch. 9; on the worship service and the Eucharist in chs. 10 and 11; [15] on the more or less extraordinary gifts of the Holy Spirit, particularly the phenomenon of " speaking in tongues " in chs. 12 to 14. The answer for all these questions is submit-

[15] Chapter 11 contains a narrative of the institution of the Holy Supper which, in spite of differences, has the same origin as the parallel narratives in the Synoptic Gospels — the oral tradition of the early community.

ted to the principle of love, which is the special subject of ch. 13. Chapter 15, perhaps the most important, deals with the resurrection, first that of Christ, quoting one of the very oldest credos that enumerates all the appearances of the Resurrected One, then that of the Christians — resurrection not of the flesh but of the body, transformed into a " spiritual body."

This epistle, therefore, is one of the most precious, both for the doctrine of the church and for the knowledge it gives concerning the everyday life of the communities founded by Paul.

It was at Ephesus (ch. 16:8) that Paul wrote this epistle, when he was getting ready to leave this city, probably shortly after Easter (ch. 5:7-8), since he is already gone when Pentecost comes around (ch. 16:8) in the spring of the year 55.

3. *The Second Epistle to the Corinthians.* The style of the second epistle to the Corinthians betrays the author's emotion, and this also makes it difficult to translate. It is the most personal of the apostle's letters. Paul, assailed, feels himself obliged to present his own defense or rather that of his apostleship.

Very precise events have taken place since he wrote the first epistle. A few indications enable us to reconstruct these events, otherwise unknown. Paul has interrupted his long stay at Ephesus to go visit the Corinthians, and he is getting ready to make them another visit (this is clear from a comparison of II Cor. 2:1; 12:14; and 13:1-2). During his last stay, he was insulted, personally and seriously, by a member of the community (cf. chs. 2:5-11; 7:12). Upon returning to Ephesus, he sent a letter to the Corinthians, asking that the offender be punished. This letter is mentioned in chs. 2:3-4, 9; 7:8, 12. It is usually called the " tear-filled epistle," since the apostle himself says: " For I wrote you out of much affliction and anguish of heart and with many tears " (ch. 2:4). This epistle cannot be our I Corinthians, which does not fit the definition of a " tear-filled epistle." The letter in question has therefore been lost,[16] the third of the four that Paul wrote to the Corinthians. Perhaps it was Titus, one of Paul's disciples, who delivered it. In any case, the apostle did send Titus to Corinth, and he calmed them down, re-established unity, and has just brought Paul back good news (ch. 7:6-16), who now takes pen in hand again.

Where is Paul now? He has left Ephesus and is going to Troas where he will prepare his last trip to Jerusalem. He travels through the region of Macedonia "giving them much encouragement" (Acts 20:2). He organizes the offering for Jerusalem that is dear to him because it is a sign of unity in the church; he dedicates two whole chapters (II Cor., chs. 8 and 9) to the exposition of the theological basis for this offering. It is in this Macedonian region (cf. chs. 1:16 and 7:5) that the second epistle to the Corinthians was written, at the end of the year 55.

The biographical details that he gives help us to know the life and personality of the apostle. He speaks himself of the tribulations that he endured at Ephesus (ch. 11:23-27), of his vision and of his malady (ch. 12:1-10), of how he regards his ministry and of the nature of his authority (chs. 6:1-10 and 10:1-11).

4. *The Epistle to the Romans.* The epistle to the Romans is much more a theological treatise than a letter. It has held an extremely important place throughout the history of the church as a guarantee of authentic Christian faith. It was used by Augustine as a weapon in his

---

[16] Some have claimed that it is found in chs. 10 to 13 of our " Second Corinthians," which in that case would have been added to the epistle after its writing. This hypothesis is hard to prove.

struggle with Pelagius; the Reformers Luther and Calvin made of it the rampart of truth; and in our day the ringing commentary of the Swiss theologian Karl Barth has given a new scope to theological thought.

Paul is here writing to a church he did not found (cf. Rom. 15:20). He now plans to go west. He has had the time to elaborate his thought in the polemics and experiences he has met up with everywhere he has been. Does he think that the West has the same problems as the East? Indeed, before even making the acquaintance of the church at Rome, he sends them an exposition of his theology. For he wants to make Rome his home base for evangelization in the West, and he already has his eye on evangelizing Spain (ch. 15:23-33).

Paul is at Corinth; he is enjoying the calm necessary for successfully completing a doctrinal exposition. He has no direct relationship with the Christians in Rome and although he takes into account the situation and the peculiar problems of their community concerning which he has been informed, he goes beyond the horizons of the local church and writes for all Christians.

Contemporary documents enable us to understand the profile and the situation of this church. We will not describe the Rome of Paul's time; there is an abundance of books on this subject. Let us only note that the Jewish colony at Rome was very large, especially since Pompey had brought a great many Jewish slaves there in 61 B.C., who had afterwards been liberated (see the short note in Acts 6:9, which mentions their presence at Jerusalem). It is in the midst of this colony that the Christian faith sprang up and developed.

We can guess how this Roman church may have been born. It was probably the result of natural expansion, since all roads led to Rome, capital of the Empire. The

Palestinian Jews streamed there to join their fellow believers. We can therefore suppose that part of these Jews who had been reached by the new faith while still in Palestine,[17] had taken the gospel to Roman Jewry. Thus it is not necessary to bring in the mission of an apostle.

But tradition associates the origin of Roman Christianity with the apostle Peter. In fact, no New Testament writing suggests that Peter was its founder.[18] It is another problem whether or not he went there later on, toward the end of his life, when the Christian community was already in existence. According to the First Letter of Clement of Rome, a Christian writing from the year 96, it is possible to suppose that Peter died a martyr's death at Rome in the persecution launched by Nero. However, in spite of the prudence required by the use of arguments *ex silentio*, we must acknowledge that the absence of any allusion whatsoever to Peter in the epistle to the Romans would be astonishing if he was occupying a place in the church of the capital when this letter was written. The Roman historian Suetonius informs us indirectly that under the emperor Claudius there were already Christians at Rome. In 49, an edict issued by this emperor ordered the expulsion of the Jews from the capital city. This edict was meant to put an end to the trouble brought on, writes Suetonius, under the impetus of one " Chrestus " (Suetonius, *Vit. Claud.*, 25). It is probable that the expansion of the Christian faith among the Jews was the cause of this trouble (we have seen that throughout the East this development was not without clashes) and that the " Chrestus " in question is no one else but "Christus," Je-

[17] Or else Roman Jews, returned from a pilgrimage to Jerusalem (cf. Acts 2:5–10).
[18] In any case not Acts 12:17: " He [Peter] . . . went to another place."

sus Christ. For a long time the pagans mistook Christian for Jew.

After the edict of Claudius, the Jewish Christians also had to depart from Rome (see Acts 18:1-3), leaving in the community only the Gentile Christians not included in the expulsion order. After the death of Claudius in 54, the Jews were able to move back to Rome and the Jewish Christians with them. The readmission of the latter into a church which in their absence had become Gentile Christian probably created a certain uneasiness and tensions to which the apostle may allude discreetly in chs. 14 and 15:1-13 of our epistle to the Romans. That is why the apostle's endeavors make evident Israel's role in the history of salvation.

We can determine rather exactly the year in which this epistle was written. According to ch. 15:25, Paul is getting ready to take to Jerusalem the results of the offering collected as a sign of unity from among the Christians of Macedonia and Achaia in favor of the poor in the mother church at Jerusalem. A comparison with the book of The Acts enables us to date this. There is a particularly close agreement between our epistle and Acts 19:21: "Now after these events Paul resolved in the Spirit to pass through Macedonia and Achaia and go to Jerusalem, saying, 'After I have been there, I must also see Rome.'" The epistle to the Romans was therefore written before Easter, 56, during the three months that Paul spent, for the last time, at Corinth.

The Pauline authenticity of this epistle has never been questioned. Only ch. 16, made up of greetings, brings up the question of whether it was written for the Romans or not. For how could the apostle, never having been to Rome, know so many people who live there? Is Epaenetus, "first convert in Asia," really at Rome (Rom. 16:5)?

Aquila and Prisca had a house at Ephesus, if we take for granted I Cor. 16:19: " Aquila and Prisca, together with the church in their house, send you hearty greetings in the Lord." (Remember that the first epistle to the Corinthians was written at Ephesus.) Now, according to Rom. 16:4-5, they are to be greeted with the community meeting " in their house."

Thus, some have proposed that this ch. 16 is an epistle for Ephesus. But can an epistle contain only greetings? An examination of the ancient manuscripts suggests another explanation. The papyri Chester Beatty (known as " P[46] "), which date from the third century, put the final doxology of ch. 16:25-27 after ch. 15:33. They therefore seem to attest the existence of copies not containing ch. 16. Also, the two words " in Rome " (ch. 1:7 and 15), found in most of the ancient manuscripts, are absent in others. Of course chs. 1 to 15 of the epistle were sent to Rome, but the habit, recommended by Paul himself,[19] of passing his letters on from church to church, permits us to believe that the apostle wanted his epistle to be read by the Christians of Ephesus; for the copy to be sent to Ephesus, then, he added a short letter of greeting, which makes up ch. 16. This would explain why the address " in Rome " was taken out of the " Ephesian edition " of the epistle. This explanation commands all the more respect since the same remark can be made for the epistle to the Ephesians (which we will study farther on), in which the words " in Ephesus " in the salutation (Eph. 1:1) are missing in the best manuscripts.

The theological content is too rich to be summarized. Its subject is formulated in ch. 1:16-17: " The gospel . . . is the power of God for salvation to every one who has

[19] See below, concerning the epistle to the Colossians.

faith, to the Jew first and also to the Greek. For in it the righteousness of God is revealed through faith for faith."

The epistle to the Romans follows a systematic outline that we will try to delineate here to facilitate the reading of this Paul's masterwork. After an epistolary introduction (ch. 1:1-17), we find:

I. *Part One, doctrinal in nature*, going through to the doxology of ch. 11:36, which may be subdivided as follows:
   A. Chs. 1:18 to 8:39 — justification by faith
      1. Chs. 1:18 to 3:20 — negative aspect: without faith, Jews as well as pagans are subject to God's wrath
      2. Chs. 3:21 to 8:39 — positive aspect: Scriptural proof by Abraham's faith (ch. 4), humanity from Adam to Jesus Christ (ch. 5), baptism which enables us to participate in Christ's death and resurrection (ch. 6), the role of the law which makes sin manifest and provokes conflict in man (ch. 7), deliverance by the Holy Spirit (ch. 8)
   B. Chs. 9:1 to 11:36 — the history of salvation, Jews and pagans
II. *Part Two, with an ethical bearing*, deals with sanctification and goes from chs. 12:1 to 15:13. Chapter 13 takes up the problem of the proper attitude toward the state and ch. 14 that of the relationship of the strong and the weak in the faith.

Finally, a double conclusion is supplied by ch. 15, which contains travel plans and ends with a blessing, and by ch. 16, which we have mentioned, including a series of greetings and ending with a blessing followed by a doxology.

III. The Epistles of the Captivity

The following epistles have the common trait of having been written in prison (Phil. 1:7, 13-14; Philemon 1, 9; Eph. 3:1; 4:1; Col. 4:3, 10, 18), whence the designation for the group. In fact, since the apostle Paul was imprisoned several times the problem will be that of discovering the captivity to be assigned to each book.

1. *The Epistle to the Philippians.* The city where Paul was in prison (Phil. 1:7, 13-14) when he wrote this letter is, according to the classical hypothesis, Rome. There he was assigned to a residence guarded by a Roman soldier (Acts 28:16).

Several passages have been claimed to be in favor of this hypothesis. In Phil. 1:13, a " praetorium " is mentioned. This word can designate either a building (the imperial palace or the barracks of the praetorian guard), or a group of persons (the soldiers of this guard; this is the case for ch. 1:13: ". . . and to all the rest "). It can therefore be applied to Rome, but not exclusively. In any case, the residence of the governors of the farthest Roman provinces from the capital also bore this name. Thus the Roman governor of Caesarea lived in a praetorium built by Herod (Acts 23:35) and Pontius Pilate, while he was in Jerusalem, also lived in a praetorium (see Matt. 27:27).

In Phil. 4:22, we read: " All the saints [the Christians] greet you, especially those of Caesar's household." Is this an argument for situating in Rome this captivity of Paul? No, for the inscriptions show us that the expression " those of Caesar's household " does not designate only members of the imperial family or court, but slaves, freed slaves, soldiers, or clerks in the emperor's service, and these individuals were found in all the great cities of the Empire. That is why the " Roman " hypothesis has often been questioned. It has been claimed that Rome was too far from Philippi for people to travel back and forth fairly rapidly, as the information given by our epistle would require. This argument is not absolutely conclusive. Attempts have been made to situate the writing of this epistle in Caesarea where the apostle was put in prison. Today, Ephesus is mentioned more often, which is nevertheless conjectural, since we do not even know if Paul was imprisoned in Ephesus.

The description of the church where Paul was when writing this letter agrees rather closely with what we know about the church of Rome. What we inferred from the epistle to the Romans regarding the makeup of this community and a certain tension between Jewish Christians and Gentile Christians has to be compared with Phil. 1:12-17, and also with the First Letter of Clement to the Corinthians.

This early Christian document, written about 96 by one of the leaders of the Roman church, warns the Corinthians concerning the discord which is threatening their unity. He tells how at Rome, thirty years before, "jealousy" and "a spirit of quarreling" had made Paul and Peter suffer. The author dedicates three whole chapters to this problem to show that always, even under the old covenant, jealousy has brought on evils and even death. Here are his words concerning Paul: "It is because of jealousy and discord that Paul showed forth the price of patience. Seven times burdened with chains, banished, stoned, a herald in the east and in the west, he received for his faith a shining glory. Having taught justice to the entire world, reached the limits of the west, borne his testimony before governors, he thus left the world and went away to the holy place, an illustrious model of patience" (ch. 5).

The two Greek words *phthonos,* "jealousy," and *eris,*

" discord," which Clement of Rome uses, are found in our epistle to the Philippians in ch. 1:15: " Some indeed preach Christ from jealousy and a spirit of discord." It seems clear, then, that it is the situation of the Roman community which Paul is describing at the beginning of his epistle (vs. 12-18).

Let us also note that, according to v. 23, the apostle admits that it is possible for him to die before Christ's return, which is more easily understood toward the end of his life, therefore during the Roman captivity. In this case, the epistle to the Philippians should be dated from the year 59 or 60.

What do we know about the addressees? Philippi, a city in Macedonia, was the first European city in which Paul founded a Christian church. The book of The Acts gives in detail this founding which took place during his second missionary journey (Acts 16:8-40). This community is especially dear to the apostle's heart, and he praises it in our epistle: " I thank my God in all my remembrance of you, always in every prayer of mine for you all making my prayer with joy, thankful for your partnership in the gospel from the first day until now " (Phil. 1:3-5). That is why, contrary to his principles, he accepted personal gifts from this community (ch. 4:10-20).

Theologically, we must mention the particularly remarkable passage from ch. 2 (vs. 6-11), which gives a magnificent résumé of the doctrine of Jesus Christ " who, though he was in the form of God, . . . emptied himself." This rhythmical passage, in which the Aramaic influence has been noted (Ernst Lohmeyer), breaks into the line of thought of the epistle and uses a different vocabulary. It is very possible that we have in it one of the first liturgical hymns used by the early Christian community to sing its faith in Christ.

The invitation to "Rejoice in the Lord always" (ch. 4:4) is a characteristic sign of this epistle both intimate and profound.

2. *The Epistle to Philemon.* This epistle has only one chapter with twenty-five verses. It is an altogether personal letter sent by Paul to one Philemon, a rich man, whose slave has left him to join up with the apostle. Paul intervenes in a tactful and refined way in favor of this slave, who not only fled but robbed his master as well. This slave's name is Onesimus, meaning "useful," thus Paul, sending Onesimus back to his master, makes a play on words: "Onesimus who used to be useless, but who now is useful both for you and me!" (v. 11). Onesimus has become a Christian and Paul would like to keep him with him, but he wants to do nothing without Philemon's permission. He exhorts him to forgive Onesimus for his running away and his thievery and to look upon him, no longer as a slave, but as a brother in the faith. The apostle even promises to pay Philemon back for what he has lost.

The short message is not without a spiritual interest, for we see in it how social ethics is modified when it is considered from the standpoint of Christian faith.

The theological background is the same as that of the epistle to the Colossians which we are now going to study, which contains an exposition of the doctrine of the duties of slaves to their masters. Indeed, a close relationship exists between these two writings — the same fellow sender is mentioned: Timothy (Philemon 1 and Col. 1:1); greetings are sent from the same people (Philemon 24 and Col. 4:10-13); and Onesimus delivers the two letters (Philemon 12 and Col. 4:7-9).

Paul is a prisoner (vs. 1, 9, and 10), but he hopes to

be freed (v. 22). Which captivity is this? Probably the last in Rome toward the end of the apostle's life; Paul himself says that he is an old man (v. 9). This little letter should therefore be dated from about the year 59.

3. *The Epistle to the Colossians.* This epistle is very important theologically speaking because of its exposition of the cosmic work of Christ. It makes evident the relationship between the history of salvation in Christ and the entire creation. By thus spreading the Christian horizons out to the universe, it tackles a problem just as crucial in antiquity as in our day; and it deals with it without betraying the essence of the gospel into the hands of a philosophy.

It was written at the same time as the epistle to Philemon, about the year 59. Paul is in prison (Col. 4:3, 10, 18), probably in Rome.

Colossae, today in ruins, was a small city situated in western Phrygia on the banks of the Lycos, rather close to two important cities — Hierapolis and Laodicea (v. 13). The church at Colossae was not founded by Paul, but by one Epaphras, a "faithful minister of Christ" (ch. 1:7). The neighboring church of Laodicea was probably founded by the same person (cf. chs. 2:1 and 4:12) and the apostle recommends that the two churches exchange their respective letters: "And when this letter has been read among you, have it read also in the church of the Laodiceans; and see that you read also the letter from Laodicea" (ch. 4:16).[20] This helps us to understand how partial collections of the Pauline epistles were constituted.

---

[20] Paul therefore wrote a letter to the Laodiceans, which is today lost, unless, as is very possible, we have here the canonical epistle known as the Epistle to the Ephesians (see this problem below, pp. 84 ff.).

When the apostle writes this letter, Epaphras is with him (v. 12). He has brought good news to the apostle from the community at Colossae where faith and charity are reigning (chs. 1:4; 2:5). However, a heresy has sprung up attempting to mix philosophical speculation (ch. 2:8) tainted with Gnosticism in with the gospel. Paul counters it with the clearest Christological doctrine: " The whole fulness of deity [which is one of the heretics' subjects] dwells bodily in Christ," " you have fully everything in Christ " (vs. 9-15). This heresy is propagated by Jewish Christians, and the apostle takes care to emphasize the superiority of " spiritual circumcision " over the fleshly circumcision of Judaism (v. 11); finally, these heretics are trying to introduce ascetic practices which Paul impugns, in spite of their appearance of wisdom, as being contrary to Christian liberty (vs. 16-23). Then he describes the true discipline of the Christian life (chs. 3:1 to 4:6).

The apostle is personally acquainted neither with the Colossians nor with the Laodiceans (ch. 2:1), and no attack has been made on his teaching; why, then, is he writing to these two communities? Epaphras, himself powerless before the explosion of this heresy, probably asked him personally to intervene. Paul wants to encourage this young church to stay firm in the faith (vs. 6-7) and reminds it of the absolute incompatibility of the gospel with the philosophical ideas some would like to mix in with it.

The epistle to the Colossians is considered to be inauthentic by many critics for the following three main reasons:

a. It combats Gnostic doctrines, whereas Gnosticism [21]

[21] Gnosticism, an intellectualistic theological movement, is founded on gnosis or knowledge (in Greek, *gnôsis*). At its beginning it

did not appear before the second century, which would move the origin of this epistle up to the second century;

b. The doctrine concerning Christ that is here set forth goes far beyond the developments of the other Pauline epistles. In particular, Christ's participation in the creation of the world is an idea in disagreement with the rest of the Pauline Christology;

c. The vocabulary and style are very different from those of the other epistles;

d. The epistle shows a curious similarity to the epistle to the Ephesians, a similarity which could suggest its dependence on the latter.

What are these arguments worth?

a. It is inexact to claim that Gnosticism did not appear before the second century. Preliminary forms of it can be shown to exist in certain currents of Judaic thought. Gnosticism did not assail Christianity for the first time in the direct confrontation of Christian thought with Greek thought, but previously and indirectly by Hellenized Judaism;

b. Christ's preexistence is not an idea peculiar to this epistle; we find it expressed in the epistle to the Philippians (ch. 2:9-11). The participation of Christ in the creation of the world even appears in I Cor. 8:6, and the authenticity of this passage has never been questioned;

c. If Paul wants to combat the Gnostics effectually, he must fight with them on their own ground, and use Gnostic terms to turn them on their authors;

d. The problem of the similarity to the epistle to the

---

was a simple intellectual tendency to consider metaphysical speculation as the most important part of the Christian faith. Then Gnosticism was fixed in Gnostic systems, and elements foreign to Christian theology were added in. But today many are of the opinion that the origin of Gnosticism should be set back beyond that of Christianity.

Ephesians can in no case be solved in the sense of the epistle to the Colossians being dependent on Ephesians. Indeed, the parallel passages seem to be earlier in the epistle to the Colossians.

Since no truly definitive argument can be brought to bear on the Pauline authenticity of this epistle, we consider it, therefore, to be from the pen of the apostle Paul.

4. *The Epistle to the Ephesians.* The central doctrine of the epistle to the Ephesians is ecclesiological, that is, its subject is the church and Christ's relationship with her. The church is to Christ as the body is to the head (Eph. 1:23), as the wife is to the husband (ch. 5:23-32). In our epistle, this teaching is placed in a cosmic setting, just as the epistle to the Colossians did for the person and the work of Christ.

After the doctrinal part (chs. 1 to 3), which reaffirms, in this setting, the salvation offered by grace to all men, Jews and pagans, an ethical part (chs. 4 to 6) is added as a reminder that the unity of faith, holiness, personal and social morality, and the spiritual " arms " of the believer must be within the church (ch. 6:10 ff.).

Is the church established at Ephesus, a well-known port of Asia Minor, the real addressee of this letter? We have already mentioned that the oldest Greek manuscripts of the New Testament do not contain the words " in Ephesus " in the salutation of the epistle (ch. 1:1). Even more, the apostle is writing to a church with which he is not personally acquainted: " I have heard of your faith " (v. 15). Now the community of the Ephesians is perfectly well known to him. His stay at Ephesus, fruitful in events, is recounted in detail in the book of The Acts (Acts 18:19 to 20:1), and Paul alludes to it himself in I Cor. 15:32 and 16:8 (this epistle was written in Ephesus, as we have already seen). Another indication, Mar-

cion, a heretic from Asia Minor who settled down in
Rome about 140 and who was the first to give a title to
the Pauline epistles, entitles this one "Epistle to the
Laodiceans." Even if, doctrinally speaking, we have every reason to distrust Marcion, on the other hand, for
this historical problem, we have no reason for being
skeptical.

We are able to guess why the salutation is not found in
the oldest manuscripts, when we remember that even
during Paul's lifetime, and encouraged by him, an exchange of letters took place between churches. We have
seen that the problem of ch. 16 of the epistle to the Romans is explained in this way. Thus we understand how,
since it was read in different churches, this epistle in the
end lost the name of the original addressee. The similarity between our epistle to the Ephesians and the epistle to the Colossians would be explained if the former
had first been addressed to the Laodiceans. They both
were written at the same time, and our letter was first
exchanged with the Colossians on the recommendation of
the apostle himself (cf. Col. 4:16). Our epistle to the
Ephesians in this case would be this letter written to the
Laodiceans, according to Col. 4:16, and generally thought
to be lost. This would also explain why the same person,
Tychicus, mentioned in Col. 4:7 and in Eph. 6:21, delivered both letters, since Colossae and Laodicea were
neighboring cities. We could even guess why, afterwards,
the name of Laodicea fell definitively from use, the result
of a false conclusion drawn from a passage taken from
the Johannine apocalypse. This book contains, among its
seven letters to the churches in Asia, a letter to the
church at Laodicea, and the resurrected Christ says, "I
will spew you out of my mouth" (Rev. 3:16).

But we still have to explain why the words "in Ephesus" have been retained in most of the manuscripts. A copy of our epistle, let us say, was received in Ephesus. We have already seen that, before reading the letter to the communities gathered together for the worship service, the name of the city in the salutation was changed. The words "in Ephesus," written in the copy which was read there, were not removed from the copies sent elsewhere, and all the more so since the need was felt of having a letter carrying the name of the church where Paul had stayed longer than anywhere else.

However, the Pauline authenticity of our epistle has been severely questioned.

Most modern critics vote against it. These are the reasons given:

a. The too great similarity with the epistle to the Colossians would make such a repetition by the same author inconceivable. It must be added that, precisely in the parallel passages, the epistle to the Ephesians uses in several places a different vocabulary from that of the epistle to the Colossians;

b. Generally speaking, the vocabulary here is not the same as in the other epistles — for example, in Eph. 4:27, the devil is called *diabolos* instead of the usual *Satanas;*

c. The theological conceptions are more developed; whereas Col. 1:26 speaks of the "saints," a term commonly applied from the beginning to all the Christians, the parallel passage of Eph. 3:5 mentions "the holy apostles and prophets" and thus gives the word its later meaning;

d. The organized church was provided with "ministers," which this epistle presupposes did not as yet exist in Paul's time.

Without denying the worth of these arguments, we can give these answers:

a. The problems were the same in the two neighboring churches of Colossae and Laodicea, both founded by Epaphras; and it is logical that two letters sent at the same time to two communities, both unknown to the author, would be much alike. It is true that this does not explain the use of different terms, precisely in the parallel passages;

b and c. To explain the general change of vocabulary and of certain theological conceptions, we must bring into the question the fact that differences may have been the result of the apostle's using collaborators and secretaries, as we may infer from other epistles. The exact role of his collaborators should be studied more precisely;

d. The church in Paul's time is neither anarchic nor purely charismatic (that is, guided by the "charismata," gifts of the Holy Spirit). It already has organized functions, with established forms of ministry. If it lives by the breath of the Spirit, its life is not regulated by moment-to-moment inspiration. The apostleship, for example, "charismatic" as it may be, is already a governmental organ of the church whose authority is well established.

On the other hand, two arguments can be urged in favor of Pauline authenticity:

a. The external evidence is excellent since its authenticity is indirectly attested by Ignatius (Bishop of Antioch, who died a martyr in 110), Polycarp (Bishop of Smyrna around 150), and the heretic Marcion (established in Rome about 140).

b. In spite of new ecclesiological developments, the theological contents can find a place in Paul's overall theology.

We conclude that if the epistle is Paul's, it was probably destined for the church at Laodicea at the same time that the epistle to the Colossians was written, that is,

about 59. The part that the collaborator or secretary of
the apostle had in its writing seems, in any case, to be
greater than in the other epistles, and perhaps it should
be acknowledged also that after the epistle became definitively the epistle to the Ephesians, it was retouched.

The problem of the authenticity or the inauthenticity
necessitates, on the one hand, serious study of pseudepigraphy (which is the ascription of a work to an authority who is not its author) in antiquity and particularly in
ancient Christianity. On the other hand, we should become better acquainted with the precise function of the
apostle's fellow senders, collaborators, and secretaries.
The question will come up especially for the Pastoral
Epistles.

However that may be, the theological worth of our
epistle does not depend on that problem. The way in
which Christ's relationship with his church is defined
makes of it a precious element of the Biblical message.

IV. THE PASTORAL EPISTLES

There are three of these and they are entitled First
Epistle to Timothy, Second Epistle to Timothy, Epistle to
Titus. They have been given the name " pastoral " only
since the eighteenth century. In fact, this inclusive title
corresponds to their content. They are works of ecclesiastical discipline, for the care of the spiritual and material situation of the church.

The Pauline authenticity of these letters, at least in
their present form, is very uncertain. We will come back
to this hotly discussed problem. The three epistles are so
alike that we will present all three together.

The historical situation in which they were written is
hard to determine. According to I Timothy, Paul has

gone to Ephesus and then into Macedonia (ch. 1:3). According to II Timothy, he is in prison (ch. 1:8, 16) in Rome. Now as we have seen concerning the captivity spoken of in the Epistles of the Captivity and in Acts 28:30-31, Paul, although he was under arrest, was not incarcerated. In Rome he had rented a house where he received all who came to see him, preached and taught "in all liberty and without any obstacle." According to II Timothy, the apostle, to the contrary, is chained up like a criminal (ch. 2:9); during a first interrogation, he was abandoned by all (ch. 4:16), and he has no high hopes for good results in the last part of his trial and is expecting to be condemned to death (vs. 6-8, 18). Shortly before, he had visited Asia Minor and Greece; he stopped at Miletus where he left one of his disciples, Trophimus, who was sick (v. 20), and at Troas, where he forgot his cloak and some parchments at a friend's house (v. 13). From there, going by way of Corinth (v. 20), he came to Rome and now asks Timothy to come and join him (v. 9). The latter seems to be at Ephesus where heresies have spread (ch. 2:17-18). Two heretics, Hymenaeus and Philetus, claim that the resurrection has already come. (Do they teach that the soul is immortal, or that "true" Christians do not die? We have no way of knowing.) In the first epistle to Timothy heresies were already spoken of as breaking out in the community Timothy is in charge of, and these heretics seem rather clearly to be Jewish Christians with a false attachment for the Jewish law (I Tim. 1:3-7).

As for the epistle to Titus, it contains very few allusions to the historical situation which, in any case, does not seem to be the same as in the two epistles to Timothy. The only common trait is the mention of Jewish Christian heretics also enamored with Gnosticism (Titus

1:10-16; 3:9-11). Elsewhere, this epistle indicates that Paul left Titus in Crete (ch. 1:5). Thus he must be going on. He is planning to spend the winter in Nicopolis, a city in Macedonia (ch. 3:12); consequently, he is free, or about to be freed, when he writes.

What do we know about the personalities of the recipients of these epistles? Timothy is often mentioned in the Pauline epistles and in the book of The Acts. A native of Lystra, in Asia Minor, he was the son of a Jewess and a Greek (Acts 16:1); while still young, he became, after receiving circumcision because of the Jews, Paul's companion during his second missionary journey. Then Paul sent him to Athens, Thessalonica, and Corinth. His name is found in six epistles as a fellow sender, which means that perhaps, instead of being a simple secretary, he had the responsibility of writing some parts of these epistles. According to Acts 20:4, he is part of the group accompanying Paul during his last trip to Rome. This is confirmed by the Epistles of the Captivity, for the apostle writes (Phil. 2:19-23) that Timothy is at his side and that he is the only one to share his difficulties. The Pastoral Epistles add that Timothy was given the responsibility of a special mission to Asia Minor.

Titus is unknown to the book of The Acts. He must, however, have played a bigger role than Timothy, according to the Pastoral Epistles. According to Gal. 2:1-3, Paul takes Titus with him to Jerusalem to obtain the approval of the mother church for his mission to the heathen. Titus is a pagan, and therefore uncircumcised, and Paul wants the Jewish Christians to recognize the liberty that Titus and the other pagans have to be converted to Christianity without going by way of Judaism and circumcision. He accompanied Paul during his second and third missionary journeys; when the apostle sends him to

Corinth, he leaves "with new zeal and of his own accord" (II Cor. 8:16-17). He was for the apostle not only a devoted collaborator but also a very dear friend; Paul himself writes: "When I came to Troas to preach the gospel of Christ, a door was opened for me in the Lord; but my mind could not rest because I did not find my brother Titus there" (II Cor. 2:12), and again: "We were afflicted . . . but God, who comforts the downcast, comforted us by the coming of Titus" (II Cor. 7:5-6).

A *priori* it is difficult to harmonize this biographical data on Timothy and Titus with that of the Pastoral Epistles and especially to integrate the circumstances presupposed by these epistles into the chronology of Paul's life. Either the Pastoral Epistles are inauthentic and the author forged the chronological setting as well as the doctrinal contents, or else they are authentic and it must be possible to situate them in a period of Paul's life. If this second possibility is admitted, the area of choice is small, and they must be placed in a period later than all the wanderings described by the book of The Acts, that is, after Paul's two years of captivity in Rome mentioned in Acts 28:30-31. Since the captivity described by the second epistle to Timothy seems to be much more harsh than that of Acts, ch. 28, we could imagine that, liberated after a first trial, Paul again took up his missionary activity.

A journey to Spain is often placed during this period, a journey that the apostle had planned (cf. Rom. 15:24; see above, p. 71), and that the First Epistle of Clement, quoted above (see p. 77), suggests when it says of Paul that he had reached the limits of the West. According to the Muratorian Canon, the first catalog of the New Testament books made up about 180, the project was carried out. Paul then came back to Rome and was again taken prisoner, but more severely this time. He underwent a second trial that ended with his death sentence and martyrdom. The Pastoral Epistles, then, were written during this second captivity. But one difficulty remains. Although a journey is presupposed by the Pastoral Epistles, it did not take place in Spain, but in Greece, Macedonia, and Asia Minor. This journey to Spain, still hypothetical, has not therefore any relationship with the Pastoral Epistles. It is consequently very difficult to situate the events presupposed by these writings within the framework of Paul's life.

Only a relative chronology within the three epistles is possible, but it does not take us very far. Indeed, the order of their writing is not the order of succession that we find in the New Testament. Second Timothy seems to be the last (cf. II Tim. 4:7: " I have finished the race "); the epistle to Titus must be the first because of the future projects it contains. We therefore have the following order: epistle to Titus, the first epistle to Timothy, and the second epistle to Timothy.

The question remains whether these Pastoral Epistles can be attributed to Paul or not. What facts can we draw from ancient tradition? Their attestation by Christian authors is late — which means that it is poor. Marcion does not include them. Now this second-century heretic who prepared a catalog of the Biblical books by throwing out the Old Testament and all the books of the New Testament whose author was a Jewish Christian as well as all passages betraying, according to him, a Judaizing tendency, would have had no doctrinal motive for rejecting the Pastoral Epistles, for there is nothing in their ideas that could have particularly shocked him; it was therefore because he was not aware of their existence among the epistles classed in the Pauline Corpus. Their similarities to the epistles of Ignatius and to the epistle of Polycarp are satisfactorily explained by a common tradition. It is only at the end of the second century that we find the first attestation, in the Muratorian Canon (see pp. 128 f.).

We have seen that the events mentioned in these three epistles are hard to place in the context of the apostle's life, although it is not absolutely impossible to do so. On the other hand, these epistles differ more than any others in style and in vocabulary from the rest of the Pauline Corpus. Their theological conceptions mark a stage of progression posterior to that of the other epistles. The Greek word *pistis* ("faith") already designated in them "the rule of faith" (I Tim. 3:9; 6:10; II Tim. 4:7); and "sound doctrine" is often referred to (I Tim. 1:10; II Tim. 4:3; Titus 1:9; 2:1). It is more difficult than is the case for other epistles to ascribe such peculiarities to a secretary.

Still against their authenticity has been brought up the fact that they combat Gnosticism. But as we have already asserted concerning the epistle to the Colossians, Gnosticism existed well before the second century. This argument, therefore, does not have the same value as the others.

The final and most strenuous objection is that the Pastoral Epistles reflect an ecclesiastical organization in which all the elements of the monarchical episcopacy is found as it was developed in Catholicism during the following centuries. This organization is posterior to the first century; it is at a stage of development not known to the first generation of Christians. The strength of this argument is at least weakened if we remark that the writings of Ignatius of Antioch (died, 110), in which the organization of the churches appears only in the form, well pronounced and understood already to be ancient, of monarchical episcopacy, were written only fifty years after the Pauline epistles.

For all these reasons, it is generally thought that at the end of the first century or at the beginning of the second, a Christian who admired Paul and took his inspiration from his epistles tried to establish for his time, ascribing to Paul the recommendations of these three epistles, what seemed to him to be the apostle's spiritual legacy destined for the future church. This solution, although it is hypothetical, accounts more successfully for the difficulties which we have pointed out. Is it possible, with this explanation, to ascribe at least the indirect authorship of these epistles to Paul? Ascribing them to one of his secretaries or collaborators, as we have seen, is harder to accept than for the epistle to the Ephesians, because even the period of their writing seems to be posterior to Paul. But, on the other hand, what we said in our conclusion on the epistle to the Ephesians concerning pseudepigraphy (see above) is valid here also. In particular, can we regard the very realistic references to the cloak and parchments forgotten at a friend's house in Troas (II Tim. 4:13), even taking into consideration how the ancients used pseudepigraphy, as literary fiction? Is it not possible that the author at the end of the first or at the beginning of the second century may have utilized fragments of authentic letters written by the apostle? This cannot be excluded. But in this case, it is difficult to separate these fragments from the rest of each epistle, so that even this solution does not give us certainty.

If, to conclude, we have to acknowledge that in this area we are limited to hypotheses, it is nevertheless sure that even if the instructions given to the churches and their leaders in the Pastoral Epistles do not come from Paul's time, they can still be considered as an application of the Pauline teachings to a necessarily changed situation at the beginning of the second century.

Chapter 6

The Epistle to the Hebrews

The problem of authenticity does not even come up for this work. For it does not claim, either in its title bequeathed by ancient tradition or in any text whatsoever, to have been written by Paul, as do the Pastoral Epistles. This anonymous writing was nevertheless considered, first by the Western Church then by the Eastern, to have a Pauline origin, and this is why it was accepted into the canon. Today even Catholic exegetes, in spite of a 1914 decree from the Biblical Commission (indicating "indirect" Pauline origin), may ascribe it to another author.

It is not, properly speaking, an epistle, but rather a doctrinal exposition or a sermon, the central theme of which is the priesthood of Christ.

It differs from the Pauline epistles in that the exhortations do not come only at the end, as general conclusions, but they conclude each section of the exposition.

The successive subjects as developed are as follows: (a) the superiority of Jesus Christ, Son of God, over the angels (chs. 1 and 2), then over Moses (ch. 3); (b) the superiority of Christ's priesthood over that of the Jewish high priest (chs. 5 to 7); (c) the superiority of the heavenly sanctuary, where Christ entered when he ascended, over the temple of the Jews (chs. 8 and 9); (d) the superiority of the crucified Christ's unique sacrifice over the renewed animal sacrifices of the Old Testament (ch. 10). Chapter 11 boldly paints a magnificent fresco of holy history, exalting the faith which animated the ancestors of the Jewish people. The epilogue (ch. 13) gives the work an epistolary turn and includes news, wishes, and greetings.

The title " to the Hebrews " does not appear before the second half of the second century in the writings of Pantaenus of Alexandria and Tertullian. It is the analysis of the contents of the epistle that prompted the ancient church to give it this title. Indeed, at first reading the addressees seem to be Jewish Christian. Some have even thought they could be found in the Jewish milieu of the sect known to us by the Dead Sea Scrolls (Spicq, Kosmala). Even if they had been under the influence of this sect, those to whom the author is writing are Christians, Christians threatened from all sides. From the inside, perhaps by the danger of falling into Judaism, but especially by the weakening of the first faith and fidelity. From the outside, by the spread of persecution threatening them again.

Where are the addressees? The expression found in Heb. 13:24, " Those who come from Italy send you greetings," is ambiguous; it may be understood to mean the Christians who live in Italy sending greetings to the faraway readers of the epistle, or those exiled from Italy greeting their brothers who have stayed in Rome during the persecution. The fact that it is the Bishop of Rome, Clement, who first quotes The Epistle to the Hebrews in his writings is rather in favor of the second hypothesis.

As for the date, it is useless to try to date it precisely. The persecution under Domitian seems to be raging. We propose the following limit dates: before the year 96, when Clement of Rome quotes from it, after the year 64, when Nero sets off the first persecution, since the recipients have already been persecuted. The probable mean date would therefore be situated between 80 and 90, during Domitian's persecution.

Who might its author be? Although the Pauline ideas are familiar to it, the terminology and the style of the epistle make it impossible to ascribe it to Paul. Many proposals have been made. Tertullian [22] preferred Barnabas, Paul's companion according to chs. 13 to 15 of the book of The Acts. Luther thought of Apollos of Alexandria [23]; this hypothesis has also been defended in our day, because of the close relationship between the ideas of the author of Hebrews and those of Philo of Alexandria.[24] Since the influence of Philo's ideas on The Epistle to the Hebrews is probable, naturally first thought went to an author who came from a similar environment, but it is not necessary to identify him with someone already known from other sources. Aquila [25] and even Prisca, Luke, Clement of Rome, or Silas [26] have all been put forward.

We can say only this: the author is a Christian scholar of Jewish extraction who has not only mastered Greek better than the other New Testament authors but has also

[22] The first Latin author, born about 160.

[23] We introduced Apollos when studying The First Epistle to the Corinthians; see above, Chapter 5.

[24] Born in Alexandria about 20 B.C., died about A.D. 40, Philo, author of many philosophico-theological works, produced the most elaborate attempt ever made by a Jew to rethink his faith in Greek categories.

[25] A Jew from Pontus, exiled from Rome with his wife Prisca by the edict of Claudius in 49, Aquila settled down in Corinth where he wove tents with the apostle Paul whose profession was tentmaking; see above, p. 74.

[26] One of Paul's traveling companions according to Acts 15:22 to 18:5.

made Greek culture his own. He quotes the Old Testament profusely in its Greek translation (known as the Septuagint) current among the dispersed Greek-speaking Jews. His piety is entirely centered in Jesus Christ, who for him is a living person, and his speculations never leave theology to become purely philosophical, as Philo of Alexandria so often does. He emphasizes equally well Christ's *divinity:* " Thou . . . didst found the earth in the beginning, and the heavens are the work of thy hands. . . . Thou art the same, and thy years will never end " (ch. 1:10-12), and his *humanity:* " For we have not a high priest who is unable to sympathize with our weaknesses, but one who in every respect has been tempted as we are " (ch. 4:15); he cried out and wept in Gethsemane (ch. 5:7).

Theologically, The Epistle to the Hebrews seems to belong to the same kind of early Christianity as the Johannine Gospel and epistles, which it resembles greatly. In this case, the author would be close to the Palestinian Hellenists of the book of The Acts (see above). Together with the Johannine Gospel, it is, of the twenty-seven books of the New Testament, the one that does the most to make us understand that Jesus Christ is the present master who is interceding for us, the high point and the key of the whole Bible, and that his earthly life is the central and determinant event of the history of salvation and of the history of the world (" Christ is the same yesterday and today and for ever," Heb. 13:8).

Chapter 7

The Catholic Epistles

Seven works are grouped under this title: The Epistle of James, The First and Second Epistles of Peter, The First, Second, and Third Epistles of John, and The Epistle of Jude. These seven letters are so little alike that their being gathered into a distinct group can only be ascribed to the fact that they were not written by Paul. In the Greek Church's New Testament they precede, in the Latin Church's they follow the Pauline epistles.

The appellation "Catholic Epistles" hardly appears before the third century; it can be found applied to one or another of them in the writings of Origen [27] and his disciple Dionysius [28]; in the fourth century it designates the entire group and is definitively fixed by the church historian Eusebius of Caesarea and Jerome, translator of the Bible into Latin.

The original meaning of this appellation eludes us; it is usually understood as expressing the "universal" intention of these letters ("catholic" is the transcription of the Greek word *katholikos*, which means "universal"). But in fact, even if this explanation is valid for The Epistle of James: "To the twelve tribes in the Dispersion:

[27] Christian philosopher and theologian from Alexandria, born about 185.
[28] Dionysius of Alexandria, died about 264.

Greeting" (James 1:1), for I Peter: "To the exiles of the Dispersion in Pontus, Galatia, Cappadocia, Asia, and Bithynia . . ." (I Peter 1:1), for The Second Epistle of Peter: "To those who have obtained a faith of equal standing with ours" (II Peter 1:1), for The Epistle of Jude: "To those who are called, beloved in God the Father and kept for Jesus Christ" (Jude 1), and for I John, which does not even have a salutation, it no longer works for John's second epistle: "To the elect Kyria and her children" (II John 1), or for III John: "To the beloved Gaius" (III John 1). It can, however, be admitted that these last two letters, which are after all very short, were added on to the group as simple appendixes, and perhaps to reach the number seven.[29]

However that may be, even if the title "universal" is not exactly fitting for all these epistles, it expresses in its own way a theological idea fundamental to the interpretation of the New Testament. All the New Testament writings, even when their recipients are local or individual churches, are really meant for all believers. It is in this sense that the twenty-seven books are Holy Scripture and the principle of life for the believers. The first Christian community understood this very well, and they passed them around among the churches, whoever the original addressees may have been.

I. THE EPISTLE OF JAMES

We are here in a literary and theological world entirely different from that of the other epistles. The Epistle of

[29] Just as in the book of Revelation seven letters are addressed to the seven churches of Asia, Rev. 2:1 to 3:22 (see below, p. 121), and twice seven Pauline epistles were admitted to the canon, and the churches written to by Paul add up to seven. Indeed, the figure seven, one of the most important figures in Biblical arithmology, indicates plenitude or totality.

James is not a genuine letter. Its salutation to the twelve tribes of the Dispersion is nothing if not vague.

The main question that comes up about this epistle is whether or not, at the beginning, it was Jewish or Christian. For the most astonishing thing about it is that the redemptive work of Christ is left in complete silence. Jesus Christ is only mentioned in two verses (chs. 1:1 and 2:1), and these two could easily be taken out without changing anything of the contents of the overall text which, at first glance, seems to be moralizing, Judaizing, and without a mark of Christianity.

Some critics have therefore supposed that we have in it a Jewish work for teaching morality, composed during the first half of the first century in the Hellenistic synagogue milieu,[30] and later adopted by a Christian who Christianized it by twice inserting the name of Jesus Christ (Massebieau and Spitta).

For Arnold Meyer, who in 1930 put this hypothesis into a more exact form, the "James" of ch. 1:1, in Greek *Iakōbou*, is not James the brother of Jesus (cf. Matt. 13:55; Mark 6:3; Acts 12:17; 15:13; 21:18; I Cor. 15:7; Gal. 1:19; 2:9, 12), as ancient tradition has it, but rather Jacob, the Old Testament patriarch, addressing exhortations to his twelve sons, now represented by the twelve dispersed Jewish tribes (see salutation). Each son merits an exhortation in relation with the etymology of his name. What seems to us a curious play on words was, in Judaism, a known literary genre. We do find in the Old Testament a prophetic blessing from Jacob for his twelve sons (Gen. 49:1-28), which uses this procedure, taken up again by Judaism in the Testaments of the Twelve Patriarchs and later on by the church fathers in works dedi-

---

[30] Because of similarities to certain works found in the Qumran caves, Essenian influences might possibly be present in it.

cated to the allegorical interpretation of proper names. Thanks to this procedure, Meyer thought he had found, by etymological comparisons, the successive names of the twelve patriarchs: Reuben, Simeon, and so on.

The Christian who adopted this Jewish work not only added the name of Jesus Christ, but, beforehand, he also took out the names of the twelve sons of Jacob. The advantage of this explanation is that it makes the disjointed appearance of the epistle plausible. But two parts of Meyer's hypothesis must be distinguished — the problem of the Jewish literary genre and the question of the author. Even if it were certain that it represents a Jewish literary genre, the conclusion is not automatic that the early author himself was a nonconverted Jew. A Christian of Jewish extraction could perfectly well have chosen a Jewish literary genre to develop his own ideas; such is the case with the Christian apocalypses.

But the very close parallelism between the moral ideas contained in many treatises of ethics and of wisdom in late Judaism on the one hand, and the teaching of our epistle on the other, do not prove that the author is a nonconverted Jew. In reality, he is probably a Jewish Christian. The fact that he does not speak of the salvation brought about by Jesus Christ is not conclusive. Although the characteristic of The Epistle of James is that of paraenesis (the exhortation and teaching of wisdom in a popular style), an explicit reference to the redemptive work of Jesus Christ is not indispensable. It is only necessary to compare our epistle with the paraeneses that conclude the Pauline epistles (for example, Rom. 12:1 to 15:13; Gal. 5:1 to 6:10, etc.) to see that these moral exhortations do not contain references to the work of salvation accomplished by Christ, either. But is this sufficient to claim that these Pauline paraeneses (for which we can also find parallel passages in the Qumran writings) were written by a Jew unconverted to Christ?

To prove that the author is a Christian, the polemical passage dealing with faith and works is usually cited (James 2:14-26), for this text seems to contain the attack of a Christian against the doctrine of the apostle Paul. Whereas Paul asserted: " A man is justified by faith apart from works of law" (Rom. 3:28), James wrote: "What does it profit . . . if a man says he has faith but has not works? Can his faith save him? . . . Do you want to be shown, you foolish fellow, that faith apart from works is barren? . . . You see that a man is justified by works and not by faith alone " (James 2:14, 20, 24). The most striking thing is that the same example of Abraham, used by Paul, is taken up by The Epistle of James with an opposite interpretation. Paul says (Rom. 4:3; see also Gal. 3:6): "What does the scripture say? ' Abraham believed God, and it was reckoned to him as righteousness.' " The Epistle of James seems to say the opposite: " Was not Abraham our father justified by works, when he offered his son Isaac upon the altar? You see that faith was active along with his works, and faith was completed by works, and the scripture was fulfilled which says, ' Abraham believed God, and it was reckoned to him as righteousness ' " (James 2:21 ff.). The polemic is obvious. But is Paul himself under fire?

Before this the Jews already speculated a great deal about Abraham, so that, even if the author was not a Christian, our epistle would not necessarily be a reply to Paul. If Paul is really under fire here, the author, in any case, did not understand his thought. This is confirmed by a serious comparison of Paul and James. The former stated in precise terms that what was useful for Jesus Christ was faith, but that faith was shown by works (Gal.

5:6); he spoke of the work of faith (I Thess. 1:3) and gave works, as the *fruits* of faith and of the Holy Spirit, their place in the economy of salvation. The Pauline doctrine of justification by faith does not exempt us from putting faith to work. Our author would, therefore, be contesting an erroneous comprehension of the story of Abraham and perhaps of the doctrine of Paul.

Considering the present results of research in this field, we must give up trying to identify the author of this epistle. Tradition, which we have no way of verifying, acknowledges James the brother of Jesus to be the author. Attestation for the epistle came late. No sooner than around 200 do we find Origen quoting from it, and he does not seem to be convinced that it should be accepted with the recognized books. As late as the fourth century, Eusebius numbered it with the contested books. We can only assert that the teachings of the epistle would not contradict what is known of James who, according to the book of The Acts and the Pauline epistles, for a while was leader of the mother church at Jerusalem.

Since it alludes to no historical events and cannot with surety be ascribed to a given author, it is also impossible to date this epistle. If Paul or a misunderstood Paul is under fire, which is not at all certain, it came out after the propagation of the Pauline epistles dealing with faith and works, that is, after the 60's.

Contrary to Luther's negative judgment, who called it an "epistle of straw," it has uncontestable theological worth. We find in it certain points emphasized in the Sermon on the Mount (see Matt. 5:1 to 7:29; Luke 6:20-49) and certainly a real concern for the poor. Alone, it would not give us an idea of the Christian message, but it has its place alongside of the other New Testament writings.

II. The First Epistle of Peter

Dealing with great trials and the expectation of an imminent end to the world (ch. 4:7), The First Epistle of Peter is presented in the form of an exhortation to hope (ch. 1:3-12, founded for believers on Christ's resurrection), to holiness (chs. 1:13 to 2:10, become living stones in a spiritual edifice whose cornerstone is Christ), and to good conduct (chs. 2:11 to 4:19, suffer as Christ suffered). The last chapter contains a special exhortation for the " elders," the leaders of the churches (" elders," in Greek *presbyteroi,* which became our word " priests," but with another meaning).

This epistle is addressed to the elect, foreigners of the " Dispersion " (ch. 1:1) in the provinces of Asia Minor. What is the meaning of the word as used here? It may designate the Jewish Christians outside of Palestine, the converted Jews of Pontus, Galatia, Cappadocia, Asia, and Bithynia (v. 1). But expressions like " your former ignorance " (v. 14), "You know that you were ransomed from the futile ways inherited from your fathers " (v. 18), " Once you were no people but now you are God's people " (ch. 2:10), " Let the time that is past suffice for doing what the Gentiles like to do " (ch. 4:3), are words meant for Gentile Christians. The word " Dispersion " must therefore be understood in its accepted Christian meaning. In the world, Christians are foreigners; their true place is in heaven (Phil. 3:20). This epistle claims to be from Peter, apostle of Jesus Christ (I Peter 1:1), but its Petrine authenticity brings up a certain number of problems.

1. It is written in very good Greek, with a very rich vocabulary — sixty words of this work are not found elsewhere in the New Testament. Now, what the New Testa-

ment tells us of Peter does not fit in very well with such literary elegance. Simon, whom Jesus named also *Kē-phās*,[31] was a fisherman by trade (Mark 1:16; Luke 5:2-3; John 21:3); according to John 1:44, he came from Bethsaida. This fisherman did not " go to school," and in Acts 4:13, he was considered by the tribunal of the Sanhedrin as a " common man," " uneducated." On the other hand, the epistle could not have been written first in Aramaic (the everyday language of the Palestinian people in Jesus' time), then translated into Greek, since the quotations from the Old Testament are taken directly from the Greek version, the Septuagint.

2. The absence of personal recollections concerning Jesus is pointed out, which is supposed to be surprising from one who had lived intimately with Jesus. He only says he was " a witness of the sufferings of Christ " (I Peter 5:1), but does not go into detail.[32]

3. A great similarity is noticed between the ideas of this epistle and Pauline theology. The comparable points are striking, especially with the epistle to the Romans: the figure of the stumbling stone in I Peter 2:4-8 and Rom. 9:32-33, the passage concerning the gifts of the Spirit and their use for others in I Peter 4:10-11 and Rom. 12:6-8, the recommendation to be subject to the authorities in I Peter 2:13-17 and Rom. 13:1-7. Now Paul and Peter were supposed to be theologically opposed.

4. The search, in this epistle, for the principal elements of Jesus' teaching such as " the Kingdom of God " or the " Son of man " is in vain. Is not such a lack unthinkable in such an intimate disciple of Jesus as Peter?

---

[31] An Aramaic word meaning " stone " or " rock "; the New Testament transcribes this word as *Kēphās* or translates it by *Petros*.

[32] Some have wondered also if one of Jesus' own disciples would have spoken of him in such theological terms.

These arguments are not of equal worth and must be examined closely.

1. Bethsaida, Peter's home village, is found on the east bank of the Jordan, not far from where it empties into the Lake of Gennesaret. Although this locality was Jewish, it was of a cosmopolitan nature. Andrew, Peter's brother, and Philip, also from Bethsaida according to John 1:44 and 12:21, bear Greek names which remind us of the bilingual setting. Anyone who had grown up in Bethsaida understood Greek and was familiar with Hellenic culture.

However, this birthplace would be an insufficient explanation if the part that Silvanus seems to have played were not referred to: "By Silvanus, a faithful brother as I regard him, I have written briefly to you" (I Peter 5:12). A certain literary elegance and the quotations from the Septuagint could therefore be due to this secretary rather than to the former fisherman of Bethsaida. This Silvanus, moreover, is not unknown to us. He is named in The First Epistle of Paul to the Thessalonians: "Paul, Silvanus, and Timothy, To the church of the Thessalonians" (I Thess. 1:1), and in the same way in the salutation of II Thessalonians (ch. 1:1). In the second epistle to the Corinthians, Silvanus is again mentioned (II Cor. 1:19) as preaching the gospel at Corinth. He therefore seems to have once been Paul's secretary. He is usually identified with Silas, called a prophet, companion of Paul, according to Acts 15 to 18; this Silvanus-Silas was therefore the one who really wrote out Peter's ideas.

2. The lack of references to personal recollections, instead of making us doubt the Petrine authenticity of our epistle, rather gives a sort of negative proof in favor. Indeed, the apocryphal writings,[33] to obtain acceptance and

[33] From the Greek *apokryphos,* "hidden," "secret," this word

give themselves authority, usually claimed the authorship of an apostle and included great numbers of pre-
tended personal recollections. The sobriety of our epistle,
in this respect, is in favor of its authenticity.

3. The similarity between I Peter and the Pauline epistles is very easily understood if Silvanus-Silas, who for a
long time collaborated with the apostle Paul, here puts
his writing talents at Peter's disposal; his theological formation has been too Pauline to keep Paul's ideas and
form of writing from coming to the fore here and there.

Even more, it is wrong to oppose Peter's theology to
Paul's; the two apostles are in fact closer than some have
claimed. In what is called " the incident at Antioch," told
in Gal. 2:11-12, Paul stands up to Peter because of his
cowardice, not because of his doctrine. Peter did not act
according to his theological convictions (which, concerning the question of communion of meals with the " former pagans," are the same as Paul's), and Paul blames
him only for this inconsistency.

4. An important notion from Jesus' teaching is found in
our epistle, that of the " Suffering Servant of God."

The Old Testament presents this mysterious personage,
the servant of God, who is to redeem the guilty people by
taking upon himself the faults and the sufferings of all
(see especially Isa. 52:13 to 53:12). For official Judaism,
the servant of God cannot be the expected Messiah, since
the latter is imagined to be a glorious and victorious personage, and could not possibly be a man of suffering, hu-
miliated and oppressed, " like a lamb that is led to the
slaughter." But Jesus recognized himself in the Suffering
Servant who takes the place of the guilty in order to save
them. That is the very meaning of redemption. Jesus'

designates the noncanonical books kept hidden, that is, not read
in the churches; see below, p. 126.

words represent his suffering and death as an integral part of the work he must accomplish to realize the divine plan of salvation (Mark 10:45 and the words spoken in instituting the Supper in the Synoptical texts and in I Cor. 11:24 ff.). Once Jesus even applies the prophecy of Isa., ch. 53, explicitly to himself: " For I tell you that this scripture must be fulfilled in me, 'And he was reckoned with transgressors'; for what is written about me is about to be fulfilled " (Luke 22:37 quoting Isa. 53:12).

This idea of Jesus' fulfilling the prophecy of the Suffering Servant of God comes up again in the apostle Peter's preaching as found in the book of The Acts. Although the sermons in The Acts betray the influence of Luke's theology, it is not by chance that only in those ascribed to Peter is Jesus called the servant of God (Acts 3:13, 26 — sermon before the people of Jerusalem; 4:25). It is striking that this identification, very rarely expressed in the New Testament, happens to be found precisely in The First Epistle of Peter we are now studying, which seems to indicate clearly an idea dear to this apostle who, after revolting against Jesus' suffering (Mark 8:32 ff.), seems later to have made of it the center of his theology, exactly like Paul. In fact, in this epistle several quotations from Isa., ch. 53, can be pointed out especially in I Peter 2:21-25, where the meaning of Christ's sufferings is given; they constitute the main subject of this work as far as the Christology of the servant of God is concerned.

This last point is weighty in favor not only of the Petrine authenticity of our epistle (at least for the ideas), but it also indicates its profound theological intention.

It has also been pointed out, and rightly so, that it contains elements of early Christian liturgy: traces of one of the first credos (ch. 3:18 ff., with the mention of a preaching to the dead) and of baptismal instructions are found.

In short, we can accept that the contents, if not the actual written form of this epistle, go back to the apostle Peter. It is known and acknowledged very early in the East (Polycarp, Papias), whereas in the West, it is missing in the Muratorian Canon, but is quoted at the end of the second century by Irenaeus and Tertullian.

Can it be dated independently from the question of authorship? Several very clear references to the sufferings and trials of the Christians bring to mind a historical context of slander, criminal proceedings, persecutions, all more or less openly declared, against the faithful.[34] These persecutions rage on in several places [35] but seem to be neither official nor general. It is therefore not a question of Nero's persecution, nor of Domitian's.[36]

What do we know about where the epistle was written? We read in ch. 5:13: " The elect [church] at Babylon sends you greetings."

Babylon, capital of Babylonia, with its marvelous past, whose name had kept its meaning for the Jews of a synonym for exile and oppression, still existed at this time according to Josephus and Philo; but it had lost all importance, and the Jewish colony had even left it to go settle in Seleucia about the middle of the first century. It is not likely that Peter went there. Another Babylon could yet be considered, emplacement of a military camp located by Strabo and Josephus in Egypt near the modern city of Cairo; but it is difficult to see how this more or less obscure Babylon could be that of I Peter 5:13.

---

34 I Peter 2:12, 19-21; 3:15-17; 4:4, 12-16: " If you are reproached for the name of Christ . . . ," " if one suffers as a Christian. . . ."

35 See the countries named in I Peter 1:1 and the observation in ch. 5:9.

36 But the nearer to Domitian's persecution the date of writing is set, the greater will be the chronological separation between Peter and the writer.

We still have the symbolic interpretation in which Babylon designates Rome. We have noted the silence of the New Testament concerning Peter's possible stay at Rome. This is probably the only text giving an indirect hint regarding this stay. For the use of symbolic names, taken from Judaism, was frequent with the Christians. Thus, in the book of Revelation, in ch. 17, Babylon designates Rome. The author describes the vision of a woman seated on seven hills, on her forehead is written the word " Babylon," which is to be interpreted (Rev. 17:5 ff.). This woman represents "the great city which has dominion over the kings of the earth" (ch. 17:18). We feel, therefore, that Babylon in I Peter 5:13 also designates Rome.

III. The Epistle of Jude

In our editions of the New Testament, The First Epistle of Peter is followed by a second that is also attributed to him. But we are going to see that II Peter only takes up what is furnished by The Epistle of Jude, which is therefore anterior. Thus we will first deal with The Epistle of Jude. This short work is an exhortation which, although it is addressed in a very general way to "those who are called" (that is, all Christians, v. 1), rapidly takes on a pamphleteering tone and minces no words. The author attacks those who, both dissolute and false teachers, are poisoning the life of the church. He had thought to write calmly a letter dealing with salvation (v. 3), but, learning that false teachers have crept into the community, he no longer holds himself back and expresses his indignation. Such precise polemics, after such a universal salutation, are astonishing.

The author presents himself as Jude (or Judas, the Greek name is *Ioudas*), "servant of Jesus Christ and brother of James." Is this sufficient to identify him? Several persons with this name are known in the New Testament — Judas Iscariot, the apostle who betrayed Jesus; Jude " son of James " (Luke 6:16; Acts 1:13; John 14:22) who, according to a doubtless secondary tradition,[37] was one of the twelve apostles; and, finally, a third Jude, a brother of Jesus (Matt. 13:55; Mark 6:3).

Judas Iscariot excluded, can the apostle Jude, son of James, be the one? According to Jude 17, the apostles are dead, or at least the author is not one of them. Is it Jude, brother of Jesus? Mark (ch. 6:3) mentions James as being one of Jude's brothers. The latter would therefore have a brother James, which corresponds with v. 1 of our epistle. But why, then, did the author prefer to refer to himself as the brother of James rather than as Jesus' brother? In another respect, is the composition of this letter by a brother of Jesus possible?

This epistle contains one peculiarity that must be noted, because it is interesting both for the history of the Biblical canon and for dating the epistle itself. It quotes, several times, apocryphal Judaic books and especially the Book of Enoch.

One of the quotations (Enoch 1:9) is even solemnly inserted as though it were a text from Holy Scripture (vs. 14 f.): " Enoch in the seventh generation from Adam prophesied, saying, ' Behold, the Lord came with his holy myriads. . . .'" The First Book of Enoch, or Ethiopian Enoch, is a composite Jewish work in different sections from different periods, from the second century B.C. to Jesus' time.

If our epistle quotes this work, it is because it has not as yet been separated by the Jews from the Old Testament canon. For, in the first century A.D., the list of books making up the Jewish Bible, the Christians' Old Testa-

---

[37] It can be shown that this is probably a duplication of Judas Iscariot.

ment, had not yet been decided. This was done definitively only in 90 at Jamnia, a locality on the Judean fron-
tier, about eight miles from the sea, which had become,
after the fall of Jerusalem in 70, the spiritual center of
Judaism where the generally authorized rabbis came together. After this date, the books of the Greek Bible (Septuagint) which had no Hebrew original and which were
too recent or more or less doctrinally heterodox, such as
the Book of Enoch quoted by Jude, no longer enjoyed
the same authority.

The conclusion, therefore, is that our epistle was written before 90. But on the other hand, it reveals a more
developed stage of Christian thought. We cannot, for that
reason, go much farther back than the year 90. Indeed
the apostles are spoken of as in the past (vs. 17 and 18)
and the faith as " once for all delivered to the saints "
(compare vs. 3 and 20).

The vocabulary and style show that the author knows
his Greek well (there are eleven Greek words in this epistle found neither in the New Testament nor in the Septuagint), but he is of Jewish extraction, since there are a
few Semiticisms here and there. This Jewish Christian
could therefore, from this standpoint, be the brother of
Jesus and James, but the date ascribed to the epistle
makes this identification difficult.

Other indications allow us to say that he is probably
from Syria. Veneration for Jude was in fact long-lived in
Syria, as the known ancient Syrian documents prove.

The Muratorian Canon, the oldest known list of New
Testament writings, which, as we remember, dates from
around 180, mentions The Epistle of Jude with the canonical books, which did not keep ancient writers from expressing doubts concerning it.

IV. The Second Epistle of Peter

A comparison of The Second Epistle of Peter with Jude reveals a great similarity between chs. 2 and 3 of II Peter and the twenty-five verses of Jude. The beginning salutation is almost identical (II Peter 1:2 and Jude 2); even more, the texts of II Peter 2:1 to 3:18 and Jude 3 to 25 are so parallel that they could be written in two columns like the Synoptics (see above, p. 25). The subject is the same — polemics against false teachers; the same references to the same events are given in the same order — the fall of the angels (II Peter 2:4; Jude 6), Sodom and Gomorrah (II Peter 2:6; Jude 7), Balaam (II Peter 2:15-16; Jude 11). Several verses are almost word for word alike, such as II Peter 2:12 and Jude 10. Everything is as though the author of one of the epistles had copied from the other, changing things around a little.

There is, however, an important difference: the quotations from apocryphal Old Testament books, which were abundant in The Epistle of Jude, have disappeared in II Peter. Therefore, the author of II Peter, going over the verses of Jude, eliminated them. And for what other reason than that the exclusion of the apocryphal books by the rabbinical assembly at Jamnia had come about between the two epistles?

It is therefore clear that The Second Epistle of Peter was written after 90. This granted, it is impossible that its author be Peter who, according to tradition, died around 64 or 67 at Rome during or shortly after Nero's persecution. But it claims to have been written by Peter: " Simon Peter, servant and apostle of Jesus Christ " (ch. 1:1). The author recollects (v. 18) that he knew Jesus and was with him on the Mount of Transfiguration,[38] but

[38] The episode is recounted in the Gospels: Matt. 17:1-8; Mark 9:2-8; Luke 9:28-36.

this insistence on recalling personal memories is extremely suspicious, as we have said. On the other hand, this epistle refers to I Peter and its purpose is to follow it up (II Peter 3:1).

Another indication proving that it is a late work: in ch. 3:15-16 we read: " Count the forbearance of our Lord as salvation. So also our beloved brother Paul wrote to you according to the wisdom given him, speaking of this as he does in all his letters. There are some things in them hard to understand, which the ignorant and unstable twist to their own destruction, as they do the other scriptures." The expression " all his [Paul's] letters " leads one to suppose that, at that time, the Pauline epistles were already gathered together in a " corpus," a collection. Moreover, these Pauline letters are considered as Holy Scripture, as inspired and canonical writings with the same authority as the Old Testament. This is the first time that the New Testament books are called Scriptures. Now the New Testament canon was not fixed even roughly before 150. Therefore, II Peter was written well after 90, about 150.

The Muratorian Canon (180) does not mention this epistle, but it gives Jude, which confirms that we have here a new edition, corrected and enlarged,[39] of this work. Of all the second-century writers, only Origen mentions it and then only to say that its authority is contested.

The author seems to be a Christian of Asia Minor who wants to put his brothers on their guard against Gnosticism. This heresy seems, nevertheless, to be different from what Paul fought against in the first century. Possibly the expression "the unstable who twist the scriptures " (ch. 3:16), refers to Marcion, the heretic we have already referred to.

The use of terms such as " faith " and " knowledge " is

[39] Chapter 1 on firmness in the Christian faith, and the teachings of ch. 3 on Christ's return.

entirely different from that of the first-century Christian writings; the notion of "virtue" (ch. 1:3) is altogether Hellenistic. The fact that the epistle has to react against the disappearance of the expectation of the end also proves that we are far from the origins of Christianity.

The Second Epistle of Peter is, therefore, out of the twenty-seven New Testament writings, the last to have been written, although it was accepted into the New Testament canon before some others. Between The First Epistle of Paul to the Thessalonians, written about 50, and II Peter, about one hundred years went by.

The theological worth of the book lies in its maintaining the Christian hope in spite of the tarrying of the "Parousia." [40] We learn that this tarrying, not just recently noticed, had inspired mockers to bitter remarks (ch. 3:4). Faced with this mockery, the author calls to mind that for the Lord a thousand years are as a day (v. 8) and courageously proclaims that "we wait for new heavens and a new earth in which righteousness dwells" (v. 13).

V. THE THREE EPISTLES OF JOHN

The Johannine epistles were written in a spirit of luminous contemplation. The ideas expressed do not follow a logical progression, as in the Pauline epistles, but a cyclical method. The same subjects come back several times, and everything is expressed in liturgical style. [41]

The *first* epistle, by its form and its subject matter, brings to mind many passages from the Gospel of John

---

[40] The word "Parousia" designates the return, or rather the (second) advent, of Christ.

[41] It has even been held that the whole first epistle is only a baptismal liturgy.

and especially the farewell speeches (John, chs. 14 to 17). The author does not give his name, but doubtless he is the same as that of the Fourth Gospel (this was already the opinion of Dionysius of Alexandria), or in any case, if the slight differences are taken into account, a member of the same group. The principal subjects are as follows: God is light; Jesus obtains forgiveness for the sins of the whole world; God is love; Christians, children of the God of love, are meant to love, and to love God they must love one another. There is no epistolary introduction, but a declaration that the author wants to bear testimony to his faith in Jesus, " word of life," who " was from the beginning," whom he says he " heard," saw with his eyes, " touched with his hands " (I John 1:1-4). Neither is there a conclusion, but an abrupt last word: " Little children, keep yourself from idols! " (ch. 5:21). However, the author seems to have precise readers in mind. He is acquainted with their moral and spiritual situation and the dangers they are exposed to (cf. chs. 2:12, 14, 20, 26; 3:7, 13; 4:4; 5:13).

Detailed attacks against heretics twice (chs. 2:18-19 and 4:1-6) break into the train of thought. These heretics have Docetic tendencies; they teach that Jesus had only the semblance (*dokein,* " to seem ") of a body, not a real body, and they do not believe in Christ's human nature.[42] The author gives the recipients a criterion for judging the heresy of these persons: he who does not confess that Jesus Christ came in flesh (that he became a real man) is not in the truth (ch. 4:2-3), and he reminds them of the confession of faith. These Gnostics place knowledge higher than love and claim to be without sin. The author thus emphasizes that the true gnosis, true knowledge, is subject to love. One cannot know God without loving

[42] The same problem is in the background of the Fourth Gospel.

him, nor without loving his brothers (vs. 7-21). It is not possible to situate precisely the group of Christians to whom the author is writing.

The *Second* Epistle of John takes up briefly the subject of brotherly love and the warning against heretics of the first. It opens with this salutation: " The elder to the elect Kyria, and her children " (v. 1). Who is this " elder " (*presbyteros*)? This reference reminds one of the texts of Papias concerning John the " Elder." As for " Kyria," the word can be translated by " lady ": the chosen lady is not a Christian woman, but rather a church named symbolically.

The *third* epistle is simply a personal letter to " the beloved Gaius " (v. 1). Different New Testament passages mention a Gaius (cf. Acts 19:29; 20:4; Rom. 16:23; I Cor. 1:14), but nothing allows us to assert that this is the same person. However that may be, the Elder praises him as well as Demetrius and contrasts them with Diotrephes who, probably the leader of another community, seems not to have acknowledged the authority of the Elder.

The majority of the critics believe that these three epistles are from the same author and that if the latter is not the author of the Fourth Gospel, he at least belongs to the same spiritual milieu (see above, pp. 48 and 50 ff.).

Chapter 8

Revelation

This is the book that concludes the Christian Bible. The legitimate presence of Revelation in the canon was questioned for the first time toward the end of the second century, and was especially contested in the East from the middle of the third century on. But around 150 (Justin and the Muratorian Canon), Revelation was considered to be an inspired book.

Apokalypsis means "revelation." In fact, the complete title as found in ch. 1:1 is the following: "Revelation of Jesus Christ, which God gave him to show to his servants what must soon take place; and he made it known by sending his angel to his servant John." This John claims to speak as a prophet (v. 9), and he ends the narrative of his visions with these words: "I John . . . heard and saw these things" (ch. 22:8). It is true that all these visions seem to have come from books, but this does not exclude the author's having been a visionary. Apocalypses were a traditional literary genre in Judaism.[43] To describe what

---

[43] The apocalyptic literature is abundant. We can cite the Book of Enoch, the Assumption of Moses, the Apocalyse of Baruch, the Testaments of the Twelve Patriarchs. Traces of this literary genre are also found in the Old Testament, especially in the books of Ezekiel and Daniel. Those contained in the Dead Sea Scrolls (Qumran) partially belong to this genre.

is indescribable the author naturally uses figures and borrows in particular from the Jewish apocalypses he is acquainted with. It does not seem to be possible or necessary to claim, in explaining this recourse to traditional figures and patterns, that he used Christian sources, or to reduce the book to a series of works or writings from one or several authors. He takes other figures from astrology and pagan mythology.

But he especially uses elements from the liturgy of the early church to describe coming events in the celestial sphere (for example, the last " trumpet," an instrument of worship). This use of liturgical language presupposes an essential idea of early Christianity. The service of worship is an anticipation of the end (Cullmann). It is not by chance that the author had his first vision on Sunday (ch. 1:10; this is the first Christian designation of the " Lord's day," that of Christ's resurrection), the day when the early communities gathered together for worship.

But in another way the author brings the present into his vision of the future. The book is full of historical allusions. True, it is not always possible to identify with certainty the Roman emperors in question. But it is certain that Rome ("Babylon") is mentioned, as well as emperor worship and the persecution of the church provoked by this worship. Although the " beast rising out of the sea " (ch. 13:1 ff.), which is in the dragon's (the devil's) service, represents the demoniac power that is behind every conquering empire, the author refers to the Roman Empire of his time and, more precisely, the persecution of the church under Domitian, which did a great deal for the spreading of the imperial form of worship. Unlike the Jewish apocalypses oriented toward the future only, John's Revelation is characterized by the Christian notion of time according to which the center of divine history is by anticipation already reached in Jesus Christ (M. Rissi). Thus the present time is already the time of the end, although the end itself must still be effected. The author shows the celestial aspect of present events, just as he describes the celestial aspect of future events. This is the key for understanding the whole book.

Revelation contains seven letters presumed to be dictated by the Son of man to the seven churches of Asia: Ephesus, Smyrna, Pergamum, Thyatira, Sardis, Philadelphia, and Laodicea (chs. 2 and 3). They contain references to precise situations. The treatment of these seven letters is characteristic of the intention of the author, who, with a pastoral purpose of exhorting churches in a critical situation, transposes events of his time to make their eschatological value stand out. By their number, indicating divine plenitude, these churches represent the entire church. At the same time, this representative role shows the importance of Asia Minor for Christianity at that time.

In a series of highly colored descriptions, which are not for a chronological succession of future events, but which are, as it were, dovetailed together like different illustrations of the same subject, the author describes the great drama that he must reveal: ch. 4, vision of the celestial liturgy; ch. 5, the book with seven seals; ch. 6, the opening of the first six seals (the four horsemen); ch. 7, interlude of the conquering people; chs. 8 and 9, the opening of the seventh seal, bringing on the vision of the seven angels with seven trumpets; chs. 10 and 11, interlude of the little book and the two witnesses; chs. 12 to 14, the seventh trumpet brings on the visions of the woman and the dragon, the two beasts and the judgment; chs. 15 and 16, vision of the seven plagues; chs. 17 and 18, fall of Babylon (Rome); ch. 20, Christ's thousand-year reign, the final defeat of Satan, and the Last Judgment; chs. 21 and 22, the new heavens and the new earth, and the vision of the heavenly Jerusalem.

The language of this work is very peculiar, and a special grammar for Revelation has even been worked out (Charles). It is the result, on the one hand, of the liturgical style, on the other of the Semitic influence that is felt throughout its Greek, certainly the worst of the whole New Testament. The author certainly does not belong to a Greek milieu, but is probably from Syria or Palestine.

He insists on his name — " I John " (chs. 1:9; 22:8; see also ch. 1:1 and 4) — and it is the only New Testament work ascribed to John that itself claims to be written by someone named John. He is on the isle of Patmos, west of Asia Minor, " on account of the preaching of God's word," which may mean either that he came there with the intention of preaching the gospel, or else that he was exiled there for having preached it. According to chs. 6:9 and 20:4, the second meaning must be adopted.

One segment of ancient tradition soon identified John as the apostle John, son of Zebedee, author of the Fourth Gospel. But from the end of the second century on, this opinion was questioned by some, and toward the middle of the third century, Dionysius of Alexandria wrote: " John author of Revelation is a holy man and inspired of God. But it would be difficult for me to accept that he was an apostle." Dionysius bases his opinion on a compared theological and literary analysis of this writing and of the Fourth Gospel (which he attributes personally to the apostle John). Indeed, several details show him to be right. For example, in chs. 18:20 and 21:14, John speaks of the apostles and does not seem to include himself with them. On the other hand, the vocabulary and language of our work also differ from the Johannine Gospel. How-

ever, a detailed comparison of the Fourth Gospel and
Revelation brings out analogies within the doctrinal subjects (for example, the notion of " testimony "; of the
" Lamb of God," John 1:29, 36; Rev. 5:6-14; of the " Good
Shepherd," John, ch. 10; Rev. 7:17; and of " living water," John 7:37-38; Rev. 21:6). Therefore, if we cannot come to the conclusion that the author of the two
books is identical, nevertheless, a certain resemblance
still has to be explained.

As for the date, we have the testimony of Irenaeus in
the second century. According to him Revelation was
written at the end of Domitian's reign in 96, during the
widespread, bloody persecution that was then raging
against the Christians who had refused to worship the
emperor as a god. This date is confirmed by a great many
passages (Rev. 3:10; chs. 13; 17:6; 18:24; 19:2; 20:4).

The book of Revelation always has been and even to
our day, on one hand, the object of exaggerated consideration (especially among certain sects that by a complete misunderstanding of its historical character use it
to calculate the date of the end), and on the other, of a
decided aversion (in antiquity within the Eastern
Church, later on from Luther, because the nature of its
hope was too concrete for him). It deserves neither of
them. In any case, it contains a particularly important
message at the end of the New Testament and of the
whole Bible (" Come, Lord Jesus," ch. 22:20). It reminds us of the goal of the entire history of salvation,
subject of both Old and New Testaments. By placing all
time stretching from Christ's first coming to the end in
the Christian concept of time, where the present is re-
garded as the final period of time determined by the
work of Christ, it is still extremely modern. Without au-
thorizing us to undertake calculations, it enables us to

understand present events in this light. It would suffice to read the vigorous ch. 13, concerning the conquering empire and the totalitarian ideology, to find just how close this writing is to us, although it speaks of the Roman Empire and its imperial form of worship. It is also modern in the sense that it proclaims the cosmic outreach of the work of salvation and Christ's reign, as well as the hope of a new creation.

PART THREE: THE FORMATION OF THE NEW TESTAMENT CANON[44]

When the twenty-seven works were written, they were not yet "Holy Scripture." As we have said, the Holy Scripture for the New Testament authors was the Old Testament.[45] When they introduce quotations by the words, "So that what was written might be fulfilled," they only refer to the Old Testament. It is true that the apostle Paul occasionally recalls words of Jesus (I Cor. 7:10; 9:14 and the narrative in ch. 11:23 ff.; I Thess. 4:15), but he takes them from oral tradition and not from any writings, since the Gospels did not yet exist in his time. In that case, he usually uses the introductory words, "the Lord said," and the same is true for all Christian authors up to the beginning of the second century. (See also Acts 20:35.)

It was only in works written around 140–150, the Epistle of Barnabas and the Second Epistle of Clement, that one of Christ's statements was quoted as Holy Scripture (Barn. 4:14 = Matt. 22:14; II Clem. 2:4 = Matt. 9:13). About the same time, the term " gospel," which up until then had designated the preaching of the good news, began to be used with the meaning of " book " (Justin Martyr, about 150, for example; but the latter, writing to cultured pagans, also uses the parallel but rather inappropriate literary term "memoirs of the apostles ").

Around the middle of the second century, our four

[44] Canon, in Greek *kanōn,* first meant the stalk of a reed, then a ruler, then a standard.
[45] The only exception: II Peter 3:16 which considers the letters of Paul as Holy Scripture (cf. above, p. 115), but we have said that II Peter is very late.

Gospels were not yet the only ones considered authoritative. Other gospels, "apocryphal," giving partly legends (especially concerning the periods of Christ's life not mentioned by the others), partly Gnostic speculations often ascribed to the resurrected Christ, were already widespread, and their numbers were getting ever greater. It was high time to dam up the flow. Little by little our four Gospels, before the other New Testament writings, were separated and vested with normative authority. Toward the end of the second century, Irenaeus was already trying to explain why there should be neither more nor less than four Gospels.

As for Paul's epistles, we have already seen that while he was still living and by his own recommendation (Col. 4:16), some of them were exchanged between different churches; that was the origin of the *collection,* or corpus, of the Pauline epistles. The first collection of this kind seems to have been made up at Corinth. That is why the oldest list of canonical books, the Muratorian Canon (see below) around 180 put the epistles to the Corinthians at the head of the Pauline epistles.[46] The first quotation of a Pauline text (Eph. 4:26), considered to be Holy Scripture, appeared about 150 in the Epistle of Polycarp 12:1. About 170, the first collections of Paul's writings had sometimes ten epistles (those of the future canon, minus the Pastoral Epistles and the epistle to the Hebrews), sometimes thirteen (the epistle to the Hebrews the only one missing).

It was only little by little that other writings, The Acts of the Apostles, the Catholic Epistles, and Revelation, reached canonical dignity.

Generally speaking, the New Testament canon was not

[46] In our modern editions, the epistles are arranged in the order of decreasing size.

formed by addition, as some may think, but by *elimination*. At the beginning of the second century not only were apocryphal gospels (and The Acts) still being composed, but also a great number of other Christian writings (such as the writings of the apostolic fathers of the church), which, without any possible pretention of being original sources, still were not theoretically inferior to the writings that today are included in the New Testament.

The elaboration of the New Testament canon was therefore the fruit of a process that, until it was finally fixed, spread over several centuries. But the decisive event was the appearance of the *idea* of a canon. This important period can be placed around 140–150. It was then that the church recognized that alone she could no longer control the rapidly multiplying traditions, and she submitted all tradition to a superior norm — *apostolic* tradition, fixed within definite writings that alone might be canonical.

That is why the apostolic origin, rightly or wrongly ascribed to a writing, could not help but influence the choice. In some cases, to put a book into the canon which did not have an apostle for author, a relationship had to be established, long after, between this author and an apostle. The apostle had in the church a unique function that was not repeated — he was an eyewitness. Afterward, only writings having an apostle or the disciple of an apostle as author were presumed to guarantee the purity of the Christian testimony.

It would be wrong to believe that the canon was formed by a series of precise decisions. Rather, the books that were admitted more recently *themselves commanded acceptance* from the members of the church, and when, for example, the content of the four Gospels is compared

with that of the apocryphal gospels, one must admire the
sureness of the Christians' judgment at that time, sureness in which theology sees the work of the Holy Spirit,
present both in these writings and in the communities
receiving them.

Before trying to describe the common basis of thought
in the twenty-seven writings, let us mention the major
stages in the formation of the canon. The first canon was
the work of Marcion in about 150, who made his choice
using the overly narrow criteria of his theology. Condemned as a heretic, Marcion, whom we have already
mentioned,[47] saw a radical opposition between the God
of love and grace, Father of Jesus Christ, and the just
God of the Old Testament. Admitting no continuity between the two Testaments, he rejected the entire Old
Testament and eliminated from the New all the writings
attributed to Jewish Christian apostles or that referred
too often to the Old Testament. Since the only legitimate
apostle, according to this theory, was Paul, only one Gospel could be admitted, that of Luke, Paul's spokesman.
Thus, his canon contained only the Gospel of Luke and
ten Pauline epistles (neither the Pastoral Epistles nor the
epistle to the Hebrews).

It was partly as a reaction to this excessive and arbitrary restriction that the church fixed its canon with four
Gospels and fourteen Pauline epistles (the Pastoral Epistles and the epistle to the Hebrews finally came in as being from Paul), and to these were added The Acts, the
Catholic Epistles, and Revelation.

The first list we have representing an advanced stage
of the canon doubtless dates from the second half of the
second century. It was discovered by the librarian Mura-
tori (died, 1750) in the Ambrosian Library at Milan. Pre-

[47] See above, pp. 24, 83 f.

served in Latin, it acknowledges the four Gospels, the thirteen Pauline epistles (and thus, not the epistle to the Hebrews), and The Acts of the Apostles. The third part of the canon is therefore far from being closed. It only includes The Epistle of Jude and two Johannine epistles, but no mention is made of the two epistles of Peter, of James, or of III John. On the contrary, the Muratorian Canon admits two apocalypses, that of John and that of Peter, the latter, it is true, with certain reservations.

In the following years, the lists given by the fathers of the church give proof of much uncertainty concerning this third part. A distinction is made between the writings for which agreement has been reached (the four Gospels and most of the Pauline epistles), those the canonical worth of which is still being discussed, and those which have been entirely rejected.

Around 200, the New Testament was already very similar to ours (the canon of the Syrian Church, numbering only twenty-two books, has its own history). However, the discussions continued for a long time concerning the canonicity of the epistle to the Hebrews, contested by the Eastern Church, which had little relish for its speculative nature, and concerning Revelation which, on the contrary, the Eastern Church had a hard time acknowledging because its conceptions were considered not to be spiritual enough.

These discussions, without coming definitively to a halt, stopped in the East (except in Syria) and in the West roughly toward the end of the fourth century. The important dates are: for the East, the thirty-ninth Festal Letter of Athanasius in 367, and for the West, the Synod of Rome in 382 and the African Councils of Hippo (393) and Carthage (397).

CONCLUSION

The Common Essence
of New Testament Theological Thought

We have just studied how the twenty-seven books little by little commanded acceptance and were separated and thus made up the New Testament canon. We have already pointed out the essential theological ideas of each book. But what is the internal theological connection tying all these books together, giving the collection its *unity,* and enabling us to speak of the thought of the New Testament?

It is not easy to answer the question, for every period, every church, is tempted to make a choice and to consider essential that which satisfies its own aspirations. Thus, for example, humanism thought of the essence of the New Testament as being in the Sermon on the Mount; and the Reformation chose the doctrine of justification by faith. The whole of the New Testament is then explained in terms of a single idea.

Does a criterion exist enabling one to avoid a more or less arbitrary choice? We feel that the short phrases contained in the New Testament itself and used for summing up the faith of early Christianity before baptism, or else for the confession to be proclaimed in time of persecution, show us precisely what the authors of the New Testament themselves considered to be the center of their faith (Cullmann).

These phrases are all in agreement as to the limitation of their confession to *faith in Jesus Christ,* belief in God being only part and parcel of this. Jesus Christ is Lord and the Son of God.[48] When they are more developed, they emphasize Christ's resurrection and the *present and universal reign* of him who is " seated at the right hand of God." [49] All revelation is, therefore, seen in the light of the Christ who is ever present.

But this resurrected Christ, whose daily presence, according to the book of The Acts and the epistles, was felt by the first Christians in their communities, especially in their worship, is not simply an abstract principle. He is the same one whose earthly life and ministry are told by the Gospels — he healed the sick, forgave sins, died on the cross, and he also preached the very near coming of the Kingdom of a God who loves his " lost sheep " and who asks his children to repent and accomplish his will in a radical way, according to the spirit and not according to the letter. At the same time, this Jesus had been conscious of having the role of the Suffering Servant of God and of the Son of man who will come at the end of time to manifest the Kingdom of God.

It is the same Jesus Christ who, in the community of the believers, pursues his work. The experience and the conviction of this permanent action form the basis of the entire New Testament.

The theology of the epistles (Christ is Lord of the universe) is often opposed to the simpler preaching of Jesus

48 For example, examine the contents of these phrases in their context: " Jesus Christ is Lord," I Cor. 12:3; Phil. 2:11; and " Jesus Christ is Son of God," Acts 8:37, according to some manuscripts; Heb. 4:14; I John 4:15.
49 According to Ps. 110, which is the New Testament's most quoted Old Testament passage.

concerning the Kingdom of God. This opposition did not exist in the mind of the early Christians, who discerned a *close connection* between the teaching of the Gospels and that of the epistles. Thus faith in the Lord who is present is connected with the unique role which Jesus Christ ascribed to himself, by now speaking of the necessity of his death, now of his future role as Son of man. The main message of the epistles, a message centering on faith in the redeeming death of Christ for our sins, the prime condition for our salvation, is tied in with all that the Jesus of the Gospels taught about the pardon of God the Father, who does not take into account our merits, but rather our penitence. It is also tied in with the fact, given by the Gospels, that Jesus himself, during his ministry, did in fact pardon sins. The entire early church ethics, presupposed by the epistles and founded on the divine love revealed and fulfilled in the work of Christ, is tied in with the Gospel requisite of love for one's neighbor based on the love of God for us. The means of grace offered by the Christian church, Baptism and the Eucharist, are tied in, the first with the baptism Jesus himself received from John the Baptist and which he fulfilled on the cross, the second with the last meal taken by Christ with his disciples. The Holy Spirit, power of resurrection, who is at work in the community of believers and who enables its members to "be renewed from day to day," is tied in not only with the event of Jesus' resurrection, victory over death, but also with Jesus' miracles told by the Gospels.

What especially gives unity to the theology of all the New Testament books is their common *expectation of the end.* This hope is different from that of the Jews inasmuch as the Kingdom of God is no longer only in the future, but it is both future and present. It is now founded on faith in what has already been fulfilled in Christ. True, at the beginning of Christianity, this end was expected to be very near,[50] whereas later on the New Testament authors envisaged a longer period of time. But what is essential and common to the entire New Testament, to Jesus' teaching in the Synoptic Gospels, and to that of The Acts of the Apostles, the epistles, and Revelation, is the conviction that, with Jesus, and in spite of our ignorance of the duration separating us from its full realization, we have already entered into the final phase of the divine history of salvation.

The central event of salvation is a historical event in close relation with the history of the people of Israel, and even with the history of the world and the events of its end. This relation brings the faith of the New Testament closer to that of the Old. Both belong to the *same history of salvation,* and this " historical " nature separates them both from the religions of antiquity. This is what kept them from the lot fallen to the latter — their absorption, then their disappearance in the vast syncretism of Gnosticism, a danger recognized and combated by the authors of the New Testament.[51]

The uniting of the New and Old Testaments into one " Bible " means, on the one hand, that a divine plan has been realized, is being realized, and will be realized on one peculiar historical line, chosen by God and unfolding within general history from its beginnings to its end. It means, on the other hand, that the definitive happenings told in the New Testament are the résumé of this peculiar history, its center and its norm. Although the history of salvation was fulfilled in Christ, it continues onward in the present until the end, in ways often mysterious and

[50] See above, pp. 60, 78, 116.
[51] See above, pp. 81 f., 89, 92, 111, 117.

in a line seldom straight. The path to be taken is narrow, but it is the very nature of the divine plan of salvation in the Bible to utilize, in order to realize its purpose of salvation for all men, this narrowing down, the consequence of the theological principle of election and of substitution. The way of the divine plan is the election of a small number, then of the unique One; its goal is the universe.

The immense joy and the profound peace of the first Christians, to which the whole New Testament bears testimony, are inspired by the consciousness, common to all its authors, of being situated in the same current with all the past and all the future. A part of this history, the present time, lying between the resurrection of Christ and his return, takes all its meaning as the time of the Holy Spirit, the time of the church, the time of the preaching of the Gospel. By faith the New Testament man integrates his personal existence into this history, when and precisely where he has been placed. By our natural birth, we are part of the history of our family, of our people, and of the world; " believing " in the New Testament means to integrate oneself, in virtue of a decision of faith — a " new birth " — into this peculiar history of salvation that has Christ for meaning and apex.

Bibliography

I. GREEK TEXT

Novum Testamentum Graece, ed. by Erwin Nestle and Kurt Aland. 25th ed. Stuttgart: Priv. Württ. Bibelanstalt, 1963.

The Greek New Testament, ed. by Kurt Aland, Matthew Black, Bruce M. Metzger, and Allen Wikgren. American Bible Society, 1966.

The Text of the New Testament, by Vincent Taylor. The Macmillan Company, 1961.

The Text of the New Testament: Its Transmission, Corruption, and Restoration, by Bruce M. Metzger. Oxford University Press, 1964.

II. ENGLISH TRANSLATIONS

The Holy Bible: Revised Standard Version. Thomas Nelson & Sons, 1952.

The Jerusalem Bible, ed. by Alexander Jones. New York: Doubleday & Company, Inc., and London: Longmans, Green & Co., Ltd., 1966.

The New English Bible: New Testament. Oxford University Press and Cambridge University Press, 1961.

III. General Introductions

Introducing the New Testament, by Archibald M. Hunter. 2d ed., Revised and Enlarged. The Westminster Press, 1958.

Invitation to the New Testament, by William D. Davies. Doubleday & Company, Inc., 1966.

A New Testament History: The Story of the Emerging Church, by Floyd V. Filson. The Westminster Press, 1964.

Understanding the New Testament, by Howard Clark Kee, Franklin W. Young, and Karlfried Froehlich. 2d ed. Prentice-Hall, Inc., 1965.

IV. The Theological Thought of the New Testament

The Christology of the New Testament, by Oscar Cullmann. Rev. ed. The Westminster Press, 1964.

Introducing New Testament Theology, by Archibald M. Hunter. The Westminster Press, 1958.

New Testament Theology, by Ethelbert Stauffer. The Macmillan Company, 1955.

Salvation as History, by Oscar Cullmann. Harper & Row, Publishers, Inc., 1967.